A
POSITIVE
RESULT

A POSITIVE RESULT

One boy with Down syndrome and a mum who refused
to let others tell her what he could or couldn't achieve

JOANNE PASQUALE

First Edition 2018
First Published in the United Kingdom by Summertime Publishing
© Copyright Joanne Pasquale

ISBN 978-1-909193-99-4

Design by Joseba Attard
Cover image: iStock.com/AnikaSalsera

Summertime
Publishing

For my gang – Cliff, Sam, Lou and of course JJ.

xx

"Take the M for me and the Y for you
out of family and it all falls through."

Billy Bragg

M for Me

PRAISE FOR THIS BOOK

"Joanne Pasquale takes her reader on a heartfelt emotional journey through the pages of her book *A Positive Result*. Undoubtedly parents who have a child with Down syndrome will relate to many of the situations Joanne so openly and eloquently shares in her book. Readers unfamiliar with the journey of raising a child with different needs will hopefully come away with more awareness of the fight and challenges parents face dealing with everything from friends to the establishment.

As I began reading this book I was quickly drawn in and found it hard to put down. It was easy to connect with her as she continually fought for Jamie and all he deserves. My personal favourite memory was the dinner at home with friends and 'the look'. Joanne has a talent for painting an image so well you feel you're at their table as it's unfolding.

I found *A Positive Result* to be thought-provoking, honest and very refreshing!

Through reading Joanne's memoirs and the experiences she encounters with various people (medical staff, family, friends, schools and support service) it inevitably highlights where we are succeeding as a community, but more importantly where we have room for tremendous growth and opportunity to reflect on our value system."

Christine Elliott
Manager for the Down Syndrome Research Foundation UK *(www.dsrf-uk.org)*

"Jo shouldn't be surprised at the interest in this book, it's a rare gem, and has something for everyone to relate to. Jo's book can't change the past, but it can help shape the future, and should be given to every professional involved with screening programmes as bedtime reading.

Bringing up a child with Down syndrome in a world where disability discrimination is so entrenched that it's unrecognisable, has not been easy for anyone I've met. I laughed and cried as I read, so glad Jo stole the time over the years to write it all down. "I didn't feel brave," Jo tells us, but isn't that the essence of parenthood; it's not about feeling brave, it's about that parental bond, the one which drives us to do what we have to? Poo happens, we deal with it, and we move on. Hope that's not giving away too much of the plot?"

Lynn Murray
Down syndrome advocate with Don't Screen Us Out *(www.dontscreenusout.org)*
Saving Down syndrome *(www.savingdownsyndrome.org)*
Huffington Post blogger

~

"This extraordinary love story of a hilariously stroppy mother, her wonderful son Jamie and their firmly supportive family, will keep you hastily turning the pages from start to finish. It's a triumphant tale of an anything-but-ordinary family, who both hilariously and sometimes very sadly stumble through everyday tasks and situations, weaving their way and setting their own course. This book is witty, gritty and beautifully written, a testament to a mother's fiercely enduring love for her son, and a shining beacon of humour to those of us making our way through the fog.

You'll laugh, you'll cry, and you'll be utterly exhausted when it's over. Welcome to the world of Joanne and her fabulous family."

Sue Tulloch
Proud parent of a young man with Down syndrome

"Finally, a book about Down syndrome!

I was hooked on this raw and honest account of having a child with additional needs. The theme that stays true throughout is Jamie is just one child with additional needs and this is the story of their family. Jo doesn't hold back in sharing her frustrations at friends, anger at the system and worries for the future, but most of all, you feel the love, patience, and dedication she has for all her children.

As an educator to other educators, I recommend you read this to be less quick-to-judge parents. But also as a parent myself to a child with additional needs, I recommend this book – it will be like talking to the friend you wished you had by your side for both the achievements and challenges, the highs and lows.

It will make you feel all the emotions a good book should, but you will also walk away with knowledge that can hopefully help promote understanding and acceptance of people with additional needs. You can feel what it is like to walk a day in Jamie and Jo's shoes."

Max Simpson
Founder and Vocational Programme Coordinator, Steps with Theera
– a vocational training programme for people with special educational needs,
Bangkok, Thailand *(www.stepswiththeera.com)*

"I have worked in the field of SEN for thirty-six years, the last twenty of which have been as head teacher of Treetops School in Essex, UK.

I was honoured and humbled to be asked by Jo to write a brief review of this book. I was further humbled on many occasions throughout the book by the honesty and integrity contained in the text. Every professional – health, education or social care – should read this to better understand the world from the perspective of the parent of a child with SEN of any kind.

It has made me re-think and re-evaluate the way I work and confirmed for me that I chose the best job in the world. Our children and young adults are amazing. It is time for the wider world to understand and accept this."

Paul Smith
Head teacher, Treetops School, specialist school and college, Essex, UK
(www.treetopsschool.org)

~

"A wonderfully warm and honest account of the highs and lows of loving a child with special needs.

An excellent read for any professional person who works with young people with additional needs. A great tool to facilitate professionals in understanding some of the challenges and lifestyles of families with children who have special needs.

You will laugh and cry along with the brave journey the family have been on.

A wonderful support for new parents to show that there is light and hope at the end of the tunnel, along with the proudest of moments and achievements, and a reminder for us as educators to remove the ceiling in what young people can achieve. A must-have book for any parent or educator."

Helena Brooks
Specialist Leader of Education (SLE): Special Educational Needs, UK

CONTENTS

ACKNOWLEDGEMENTS

Firstly, and most importantly I want to thank my gang. Cliff, Samuel, Jamie and Louise. For encouraging me, supporting me, pushing me, giving me the time and space to finally put this story – our story – out there. Thank you for believing in me and allowing our personal life to be made public. I hope you are happy with the result.

Sam, Jamie and Lou, you make me feel such pride I can't even begin to find the words – and you know how I *love* to use words! Each of you are very special in your own quirky way. Never forget that.

'PMA' and a bit of hard work will see you through.

I love you all to Singers and back.

Cliff, for all of your support. For walking the 'bloody dog' when you didn't want to, for getting your own dinner, for working so hard and for giving me the space to write at all times of the day and night. For allowing me to disappear off when I needed to have some time to 'just write'. This is as much your story as mine (you may have wanted to read it all before agreeing to my publishing?!).

To my wonderful parents, Maureen and Vic, for your unfailing support, your overflowing love of all things JJ, and us all. I am so thankful. Dad, you taught me to fight for what's right and Mum you showed me how to be a mum and so much more.

My sisters Michelle and Victoria for their never-ending

cheerleading and encouragement, I couldn't have done it without you. Thanks for always being there for all of us.

My brothers-in-law and sister-in-law; Dal, Mario, 'Ni-george' and Julia, thank you for being the best in-laws a girl could ask for.

My gorgeous nieces and nephew – Jake, Talia, Tilly, Amelia and Isobel who I know, through school projects, fundraising and general "Oi, you don't say that" have been in our corner since you first heard the words Down syndrome. Keep shouting guys, we need your generation to be heard even louder!

Thank you, Pam and Caroline, two of the most talented writers I know. For being the first to encourage me to tell my story. You have heard this from the very beginning and your advice, suggestions and honest critique were invaluable in shaping this book. Not a spider in sight, but sure David won't mind eh?

My dear friends Nic and Sam (sorry you had to become Samantha for the purpose of clarity in this book, you're still Sam really) thank you for being the best there is. Without your – and your families' – love and friendship (and endless cups of tea, glasses of wine and a sherry or two) I'd be lost.

Finally, to JJ. You, my love, are much more than we could ever have imagined. Much more than an extra chromosome. Never let anyone tell you that you can't be who you want to be or do what you want to do. Keep singing and dancing, X-Factor is waiting.

"Kid you'll move mountains ..."

PREFACE

What started out as a piece of homework has developed in to a book about my life. I wrote a short story called *Bath Time*, simply as a piece about a time I felt happiness – as per our instructions at college that week. Having given up my career as a journalist I missed writing so had begun a creative writing evening course at a local college. After hearing the story, my tutor suggested I develop the idea. I was very reluctant.

Who would want to read about me and my family? We are not interesting enough.

I carried on writing and forgot about his suggestion. I then wrote the school gates (*One Small Step*) piece for a blog and realised I had more to say. At the time, and for quite a while afterwards, I thought I was writing this about Jamie. It took a long time for me to say this was as much about me as it was him.

Me, as Jamie's mum.

Me, as mum of a child with Down syndrome and two 'normal' children.

It was a story about how having Jamie has changed my – and my family's – life.

This is an honest account of the ups and downs of family life – the breakthroughs, the resentments, the fights and the victories.

Looking back, I can see it was something I needed to get off my chest. It has been extremely therapeutic and I have discovered a lot about myself, and others, through writing it. I have had to confront some feelings I had previously buried away and tackled issues I knew I was ignoring. I have also been amazed, reading back, how much I have learnt along the way. Friends, family, strangers, they have all added to it in their own way. I constantly doubted the interest in this story and have been surprised how much people do really want to know. Why? I'm not totally sure.

What I do know is it was a story that needed to be told. That needed an ending I couldn't find. A story I was passionate about with characters I really did live with. It is a story to help those who may be just starting out on their journey, or at the very least a story to help those on *our* journey understand why things are the way they are.

It explains how things are so different with a child with special needs, but also how similar they are. It has been somewhere I could rant, somewhere I could show off and somewhere I could tell it like it is.

What I want is for someone to pick up this book and be moved. Not emotionally – though that would be a bonus – but moved to think differently, or act differently. To talk about what they have read and how it made them feel. To have developed a better understanding.

I started this story for my family – to help them appreciate, accept and celebrate. So one day they could – if they wanted to – try and understand how it really was for me. I kept writing it as it gave me so much more than I expected.

I finished it and faltered. Now what? Did I really want to hand over my family – warts and all – for other people to scrutinise?

I decided, yes, for all the reasons I've explained, and more.

As a thank you and well done to us all. To hopefully encourage. But most of all, to educate and inform.

It is a story without an ending but with many, many beginnings.

Being special

When I mention to people I have a son who has special needs it provokes a variety of reactions. Some ask questions – so I tell them he has Down syndrome and we go from there. Some go on to ask what this means or is and I explain that generally it means Jamie has global developmental delay. Others just leave it there, hanging. Almost like it's a terrible illness and they don't know how to respond.

I sometimes feel uncomfortable with the term 'special needs' when referring to Jamie. Yes, he has different needs but are they 'special'? Does it suggest he's more special than other children?

Does that mean my other two children – I have an older son, Sam, and a younger daughter, Louise – do not have special needs of their own?

'Special needs' is one of those terms, as a mum of a child with additional needs, you can beat yourself up about. Most people accept it as the standard way of describing a group of people. After all, it's better than saying he is a bit slow, or worse still, backward.

However, if I say straight out, "I have a son who has Down syndrome" the reaction tends to be different. The usual response – and one most other parents of children who have Down syndrome expect – is *"Ah, they are such loving children aren't they?"*

There is a misconception that everyone who has that extra chromosome is a loving, happy, cheery soul. I used to get really irritated by this generalisation. In fact, if I'm honest, it does still annoy the hell out of me. It's such a lame thing to say. There's no substance to it and no real understanding from the other person.

I want to reply with something like: "You try seeing how loving he is at four o'clock every bloody morning," or. "No, actually, last week he kicked me because I turned off the video he wanted to watch as he needed to get to school."

Of course, I don't say any of that. I just smile and nod knowingly.

But then a friend of mine put it into perspective for me.

"What would you rather people say, Jo?" she asked one day when I expressed my annoyance at this response. "Really, people are just trying to find something nice to say. They don't mean to upset you at all."

I hadn't thought about it that way and can see her point. Now I tend to shrug it off with a flippant, "Well he's a little bugger sometimes, but yes, he is also very giving."

I am not sure how I expect people to react when I tell them I have a child with special needs – or even if they should react at all. I've thought about it and I think acknowledgement is the key. The best I can come up with is if they said something like: "Oh, that's interesting and must offer some challenges, what about your other two children, what are they like?"

Joanne Pasquale
Singapore, January 2018

CHAPTER 1

FALLING FOR YOU

I was twenty-eight when I fell pregnant with Jamie. So that's the first myth blasted out the water. I wasn't old. Cliff and I had been together for almost eight years.

We had met in our early twenties when we were each on a holiday with friends in the sunny Greek spot favoured by many youngsters in the early 1990s, Faliraki. Legend has it that I was attracted to his name (I had a slight obsession with a certain famous Cliff that most friends found hilarious, not to mention weird) but I maintain it was his dance moves. It was funny when we realised we were from towns just twenty-five kilometres away from each other in Essex.

Having grown up in the 1980s when jokes about shell suits and white stilettos were rife, we had in common the stigma that comes with being an Essex boy and girl. Cliff appeared the archetypal Essex boy in some ways – a fan of white jeans and football and he worked in the city – but his ambition, drive and manners, not to mention his lack of brashness – set him apart from the stereotype and that appealed to me.

From the start, we both were happy to let the other have their independence and were quite unconventional in many ways. Cliff was working in the city as an insurance broker, I was working in north London on a monthly DIY magazine and we were equally career minded. After a few years together we bought a house, signing up to a shared mortgage. By this point, Cliff was working hard at developing his career and had a career plan in mind. I was freelancing after years of working my way up the ranks within the editorial departments of magazines and was now doing pretty well for myself. I had just reached the end of a year-long freelance contract that had paid well, Cliff's company were looking at sending him to work in their New York office, so to us it seemed the ideal time to do our own thing for six months. I wanted to travel around Australia with my best friend, Cliff was keen to further his career abroad. So off we both went but all the while we stayed a couple. My sister and her boyfriend looked after our house and, despite most people's assumptions, we were very happy with the situation.

When we each came back from our adventures life returned to normal. I got a job at a women's weekly magazine and Cliff was back in the London office. We talked about our future and decided we'd like to try for a baby.

Sam was born in 1998. There were a few raised eyebrows as we were not married, but it just didn't seem important to us at the time – I was more anti-marriage than Cliff and as is his laid-back way, he never pushed me.

His career was just taking off and this meant he began to travel a lot. I hated that it took him away from home for periods of time and would often feel quite resentful, especially when Sam hadn't slept all night. Cliff often talked of feeling guilty about not being around enough but was also passionate about his work, so we learned to cope. When Sam was around six months, I went back to work freelancing two or three days a week which meant juggling sometimes, but we made it work. Cliff proposed the Christmas after Sam was born and we married the following September, again surprising friends and family who had got used to the idea that it wasn't our bag.

Once we were married we knew we wanted to have more children and Jamie was born fourteen months later.

I was going to re-read the diary I kept from when I was pregnant with Jamie to write this piece. To jog my memory of how I felt at the time. It was a long time ago after all. Then I thought it would be better if I write it as I see it now. I figured I could go back later and write the other version, the one where it is more emotional, rawer, and less world-weary, if necessary.

Testing times

In the early stages of my pregnancy with Jamie, I clearly remember feeling something wasn't quite right. I tried to put it down to the usual newly pregnant fears most women have, but it niggled me. It wasn't the anxiousness I remembered feeling when I was pregnant with Sam.

On my way to the first scan, I felt uncomfortable, not physically, but as if I was apprehensive about something. Since having Jamie, I've heard many other women also feel this way.

Cliff came along with me to the first scan, even though we knew at our local hospital partners were not allowed to come into the scan room until most of the scan was complete; they say it disturbs their concentration. I was expecting to go in and for Cliff to join me as soon as he was called, be told whether our dates were correct and walk away clutching our black and white image.

I remember looking at the green-grey flickering screen waiting for the sonographer to do her stuff. She was a particularly grumpy woman who seemed to have very little warmth about her. She half-explained the procedure about the nuchal scan and as I'd had it done before (it was routine at our local hospital for scans between eleven and fourteen weeks) I didn't really think anything of it.

As she probed my stomach, she suddenly stopped what she was doing.

"Do you have anyone with you?" she asked in a very matter of fact way.

I think she said there was a problem …

Or maybe she said she would like to get my husband in?

You would think I'd remember something that important, but I don't.

"The nuchal shows a high risk of Down syndrome."

I do remember she said this to me before Cliff had even made it into the room. He just caught the end of the sentence and sat down next to me looking confused and bewildered – he'd clearly been told to come in quickly.

Slim, tallish, hair greying more each year (we laughingly blame me for that) and dressed in his usual suit and tie ready for his day ahead, his presence immediately reassured me. His big square hands reached for mine. Even though this was our second child he is the kind of dad who wanted to be there for all the important stuff, so taking a morning off to come along to the ultrasound wasn't questioned.

The sonographer spoke without emotion or feeling.

"The measurement at the back of the neck shows there is a high risk the baby has Down syndrome. A one in sixty-nine chance in fact. You will need to go and see another midwife. If you get yourself ready, I'll make the arrangements." She tried to be sympathetic and reassuring but failed.

After wiping the slimy gel from my stomach, I covered up my already blooming belly and we were shown into a side room. Inside the room were two horrible flowery sofas that were supposed to make it feel homely, and a box of tissues on a cheap wooden table. We were left for what felt like ages. We didn't speak much. We were both reeling from the shock of what we'd just heard and trying to make sense of it.

A while later, another nurse came in and said we were to go and see the bereavement midwife downstairs. She was expecting us.

Her job title should have given us a clue.

Walking back through the open waiting room full of pregnant women and their partners was awful. Did they know? What were they thinking about us? How dare they carry on with their pregnancies so happily?

The nurse showed us to a waiting room outside a door that bore a sign saying 'Bereavement Midwife' and her name. I stared at that sign a lot. Cliff was trying to be very reassuring. A quiet man by nature with a strong sense of right and wrong, he is the ideal person to go to with a dilemma as he can see all angles and is usually very pragmatic.

"One in sixty-nine, that's sixty-eight chances they're wrong, it'll be fine. Let's not worry until we have to."

But I knew.

While we waited, Cliff rang my parents. We'd already been gone longer than planned and we knew they would probably be wondering what was happening. They were looking after Sam, who was two-and-a-half at the time. Both in their early sixties, my parents lived in a seaside town about a twenty-minute drive from us in Essex. They would always drop everything to look after any of their grandchildren and so had come over that morning and taken charge of Sam, who adored them. Cliff explained there may be a problem, gave them a few details and said we were waiting to see another midwife. They, of course, told him not to worry and Sam was fine.

After a long wait, a round, rosy-cheeked woman dressed in a blue uniform came out and apologised for taking so long. She invited us into her office, again with a flowery sofa and two boxes of tissues – I remember they had those awful fabric covers to disguise the box underneath. She asked me if I was okay more than once. She seemed to be surprised I wasn't in floods of tears. I felt I wasn't living up to her idea of a mum who had just been given devastating news.

She explained the scan results to us and went through what she thought were our options. With hindsight, I know they were the NHS options and not ours.

"We will send you to King's College Hospital in London for what is called a chorionic villus sampling (CVS) test. That will tell you for sure if the foetus has Down syndrome."

It was presented to us as a must-do rather than an option.

She explained the CVS was a similar procedure to an amniocentesis and would mean taking cells from the placenta.

"The cells are analysed to tell us whether the foetus has Down syndrome or not." She smiled warmly while telling us this. She also explained there was a slight risk of miscarriage, continuing, "But it is by far the best option, considering ... I will make you an appointment as soon as possible."

It felt like she was doing us a huge favour.

She told us, dependent on the results, we could then decide whether to opt for a termination. She gave us lots of leaflets offering support after termination and details of what this would entail. I felt sick. I remember asking about Down syndrome. Did she have any information we could read? She was quite vague, and it was only when I pressed her that she dug around in her filing cabinet and gave me a leaflet.

"I shouldn't really give this to you yet, we usually wait until after the test."

We were told to wait in the hospital café while she made the arrangements.

We sat in the stark café on hard plastic chairs with a cup of tea each. I looked through the leaflets and felt as if the world had shifted on its axis. Cliff didn't want to read the leaflets. In the leaflets were pictures of children with their slanted eyes and similar, but distinct, features smiling out of the pages. I read things like *'Jake was sitting up by the time he was one and was toilet trained before he started school.'*

I don't honestly remember how I felt or what was going through my mind. Numbness is all I remember.

Back in the midwife's office, she told us we had an appointment for the following day. She was trying really hard to be kind and said she would be at the end of the phone if we had any questions. In the meantime, we were to go to King's and come back to her after the results were in.

As we pulled up to our driveway, things looked very different – quite literally. My parents were outside with Sam and surrounded by tools, greenery and piles of wood. The very overgrown conifers that had previously grown at the side of our driveway were now unrecognisable.

We had moved into the house, our first house together, four years earlier before we'd married, and the conifers were on the list of things to do. But weddings, babies and work always meant we never quite reached the end of that list. My ever-helpful parents obviously decided the conifers had to be dealt with and today was the day they would do it. We had no idea they were going to do this – it was a lot of work and they must have been at it all day.

Amazing what distraction techniques we all use.

As I entered the house I remember feeling overwhelmed by it all. I didn't want to see anyone, I think because I didn't really want to talk about it. Mum put the kettle on – something my mum would always do before anything else, especially if it meant serious discussion, be it good or bad. As a family, we all use tea as a comfort, as well as a distraction and a crutch when necessary.

We sat in our living room with our tea, surrounded by the things we'd lovingly bought and acquired over our few years of living together, much of it reminders of my work as an interiors writer on women's magazines. The familiar mess of Sam's toys scattered everywhere and although it felt good to be home, I felt as if I wanted to escape too. From people mainly. But understandably my parents had questions.

"Where will you have to go for the appointment? What will they do? When will they know for sure?"

Mum. Mum, with her light brown hair always neatly permed and blow dried and usually dressed for 'doing' in jeans and a top asked the questions. Dad listened. Dad, a heavy-set man whose Italian routes were clear to see was never a big talker. But he took in more than most people realised.

Sam with his chubby face, large brown eyes and gleaming head of dark brown hair (often commented on for its mirror-like shine) clamoured for our attention. We'd been out a long time and he had lots to tell us. About cutting trees down, his lunch, going to see his cousin with Nanna, all of this said to us in quick bursts in his soft boyish voice full of excitement and innocence. His chatter filled the spaces in between questions as we drank tea. It was all very normal and completely surreal.

As soon as I could, I went upstairs to lie down. I said I was tired and everyone agreed I should rest. As I lay on the bed staring at the ceiling I could hear Mum and Cliff talking in the kitchen. Muffled voices, I couldn't make out what they were saying. I cried.

I knew.

NUCHAL TRANSLUCENCY TEST

Nuchal translucency screening, or NT screening, is a specialised routine ultrasound performed between week eleven and week thirteen of pregnancy, any later and the tissue becomes too thick to be translucent and so results are inconclusive. Foetuses with increased fluid at the base of their necks — a spot known as the nuchal fold — may have a chromosomal problem such as Down syndrome. However, the results can't tell you for sure whether your child has a chromosomal disorder, only the statistical likelihood

It's often part of routine prenatal testing and happens at your first scan.

An abnormal result on the nuchal translucency or combined screening test doesn't mean your baby has a chromosomal problem, only that he or she has an increased risk of having one. This is why many women choose to have further diagnostic testing. You may also be offered a blood test at the same time that, combined with the NT, will give a more accurate picture.

CHAPTER 2

A POSITIVE RESULT

When we arrived at King's College Hospital in London the following day, we were both very anxious. We had been told we were seeing a very famous doctor who specialised in this type of pregnancy.

Were we supposed to be pleased?

I wondered about the other women sitting there in the waiting room. Was there anyone in the same situation? Were they all waiting to hear bad news?

When it was our turn we were shown into the scanning room – much bigger and much more high-tech than the one at our local hospital. The doctor introduced himself – a small Greek man with a neat beard. His manner was reassuring. He told us while it was unlikely the result would be positive for Down syndrome, it was best to find out early so we could decide what to do.

The CVS was painful, uncomfortable and completely awful. With my growing tummy laid bare and the ice-cold ultra sound gel applied, the doctor inserted a very long needle into my stomach, all the while guided by the ultrasound scan. Attached to the needle was a syringe the size of a toothpaste tube into which the cells were collected. It reminded me of a bicycle pump. Cliff and I were watching this invasion on the screen next to my head. I kept very still, and Cliff was barely breathing next to me.

When it was over we were shown into a side room with only a single chair in it and I was given some paracetamol.

Once we were left alone I began to get very tearful. I felt very protective towards my bump. If I felt like this, then surely, he or she was feeling it too?

"I just want to go home," I told Cliff.

"We will soon, you're doing great, honestly I'll get you home as soon as we can." Cliff, with the worry showing on his angular face, seemed at a loss what to do. His quiet strength and calmness was assuring for me though. Really there was nothing either of us could do.

After a short wait that felt like hours, the doctor came in and explained the results would be with us in a week or so.

A WEEK OR SO!

CHORIONIC VILLUS SAMPLING (CVS)

A CVS is an alternative to amniocentesis carried out between weeks eleven and thirteen of pregnancy. During CVS, a sample of cells – called 'chorionic villi cells' –will be taken from the pregnant woman's placenta using either:

- transabdominal CVS – a needle is inserted through the abdomen – observed at all times by ultrasound. The needle does not enter the amniotic sac or go near the baby. The procedure is performed under local anaesthetic.

Getting away from it all

Again, my parents were looking after Sam for us. When we arrived home, and had drunk the requisite tea, somebody – I'm not sure who – came up with the idea that we, the three of us and my parents, should go away for the weekend. 'To try to take our minds off things.' Obviously, this was never going to happen, but with my parents coming along too at least they would take the pressure off us to be 'up' for Sam all the time. It would be a distraction of sorts. Sam, who had already picked up on the idea, was delighted to be going to the caravan in Norfolk that Nanna and Grandad often went to – what child doesn't love a caravan? – and that helped make our decision and lifted the mood slightly.

We spent that weekend drifting around Great Yarmouth, a typical English seaside town full of ice-cream shops, fish and chip cafés and slot machines. We took Sam to the beach, to the park, the pool. Just filling time. No one really spoke about the test or what it would mean. We all did our best to keep cheerful. My parents always smiling and chirpy, keeping spirits up for all of us, despite the fact they were probably worried sick themselves. They never asked questions – as a family we were never big on long deep conversations, instead preferring to be practical and 'do' something. We all gave Sam our full attention.

The following week, Cliff took the week off work – he knew he wouldn't be able to concentrate. He'd been steadily climbing the ranks within his insurance company for the past ten years and was well liked and respected. Thankfully his company had been very understanding once he'd explained the situation.

We waited until midweek to call the hospital, that was when the doctors had said the results would be in. I called late morning, gave my name and details and, as instructed, asked to speak to the doctor's secretary.

After years of dealing with impatient mums-to-be the secretary was used to calls like this and clearly didn't beat around the bush. In a very apathetic way she informed me the results were not back and *they* would contact *us* as and when the results were available. I assumed she meant the results were due in any moment.

The rest of the day was like waiting for your first crush to call; checking the phone was working properly, making sure no one else used the phone unless absolutely necessary, cutting calls short. Towards the end of the day, I couldn't stop myself and rang again. I could hear the impatience across the line as the officious woman explained again *they* would ring *us*. I put down the phone frustrated and chastised.

The next day every time the phone rang we jumped. We didn't go out, we didn't do much. We just waited.

The call finally came two days later, on the Friday afternoon.

"The results were inconclusive."

The same clipped voice told me the test proved one of four things: either our baby had Down syndrome; our baby had Mosaic Down syndrome; our baby had another genetic condition or – and I'm not actually sure this *was* a fourth option but remember thinking it must be – that the baby was perfectly fine and it was all going to be okay.

She told me that the hospital were now 'growing the cells' and it would be another week at least before they knew for sure.

ANOTHER WEEK!

At that point, we were beyond frustration. Not to mention completely drained by the not knowing and not being able to move forward. By coincidence we were due to go on holiday to Spain the following week with friends. Three couples who we'd met at our antenatal classes when we were pregnant with Sam. We had all supported each other through the muddled, sleep-deprived slog of the early months of being new parents. Had compared hours of sleep, dissected nappy contents and discussed puréed food. I counted two of them, Samantha and Nic, as two of my closest friends. I wasn't as close to Courtney as we had quite different personalities, but we still saw each other regularly and the holiday had been booked as a group. She was also pregnant – just a couple of months ahead of me – so we had that in common.

We thought about cancelling the holiday, but everyone convinced us it would be for the best. We thought why not.
It was to a typical tourist resort in Spain, a standard apartment in a complex of identical blocks, by a quaint town with lots of bars and restaurants and some fun things for the kids to do.

Ominously the weather was really awful pretty much as soon as we arrived and we struggled to keep positive. The resort itself wasn't ideal as we had to climb a massive great hill to get anywhere. Not easy with strollers, toddlers and two pregnant women.

But it did give us space away from home and an opportunity to talk to our friends if we needed to. I talked to Samantha and Nic about the possible result a couple of times through the week. They were understanding and let me talk, reassured me when they could, told me we would be fine no matter what, they knew we would cope. They also assured me it was okay whatever we decided; they would support us. Courtney however, the one time I asked her, made it quite clear she would go straight for a termination. I was shocked by her lack of feeling but didn't have the inclination to discuss it further with her.

Strangely, it was a conversation I had with Samantha's husband Mike I remember the most. It had been raining all morning and in a break in the weather we decided to take a walk. However, we got caught in a huge downpour soon after we had made it to the top of the hill and all had to take cover in a café. The café had a pool table inside and we had gathered around it with the kids. Whilst everyone got busy setting up a game I sat down at the far end on my own, just to catch my breath. Mike, a smiley, quiet guy who is always good natured – even when we were constantly ribbing him for his strange aversion to tomatoes and musicals – came and sat with me.

"How are you feeling, Jo. About the test I mean?" he was slightly awkward I could tell, but pushed on. "The thought of the result. You know. I guess you must be feeling pretty confused. And worried. But it'll be alright, no matter what happens." He smiled and shrugged in a way that told me he didn't really know what to say but wanted to say something.

There were no dramatic hugs or displays of emotion, he simply talked to me openly. He showed a lot of empathy that day and is one of the people to whom I will always be grateful. He didn't say much, but he said it well.

The day after we got back from Spain the call eventually came. It was late morning and Cliff and I were both at home with Sam. The phone rang, and I answered. After confirming she was speaking to the right person, the voice on the other end of the phone who sounded as if she was giving me the answers to the crossword puzzle simply said, very matter of factly; "the result was positive for Down syndrome."

Standing across the room I could feel Cliff staring at my face for signs of anything. He'd realised who it was – or what it was – from the answers I'd given at the start of the conversation. I was shaking my head in a way that suggested I didn't want to hear.

"You mustn't blame yourself you know. It's not your fault. It's just one of those things. The doctor will be in touch," the uncaring voice at the end of the line told me before hanging up.

I was crying before I put down the phone. Cliff came over to where I was sitting on the sofa and we held each other, both in tears. Time stood still then. I don't know where Sam was at this moment and honestly have no idea how I felt. Shocked is the only word I can use.

We are family

I have two sisters who at the time both lived within a short distance from us. They were waiting to hear from us and sprang into action as soon as Cliff called them that day. My eldest sister Michelle went to the local supermarket where my mum was working and told her we'd heard from the doctors. She must have guessed it wasn't the news we thought we wanted as she left work immediately. I remember asking afterwards what did she do, just walk out?

"Yes, of course I did!" she said in a way only a mum whose child is in need can.

My family all came – we're a close family like that. There when we're needed, rolling our sleeves up, putting the kettle on, helping with young ones, putting some washing on.

My mum, dad and elder sister arrived first. I felt sick as they knocked on the door. My dad, a big, gentle man with kind eyes, always awkward around big displays of emotion, hugged me without saying anything. He couldn't, I knew that. My mum who always wants to help by doing and by fixing, gave me a huge hug and then busied herself making tea and checking on Sam and keeping him entertained.

Michelle, very like my mum in many ways, hugged me and asked if I needed anything doing, could she put some washing on maybe?

I didn't know what to say to anyone.

My younger sister Victoria arrived shortly after, probably bringing something with her as is her generous nature. Maybe cakes or a treat for Sam? More hugs, more words of support.

Nobody really knew what to do, least of all me. I retreated upstairs a lot.

Later that day Cliff rang his brother Nigel who was on holiday with his wife. It took a while to get through to them. Both of Cliff's parents had passed away when he was in his twenties and with only his brother to turn to, my heart went out to him as my family fussed around. In typical brotherly fashion the conversation was short, factual and without emotion. I think

Cliff just needed to talk to him really. His brother, who was on an island in the middle of nowhere with a bad signal, promised to call when he was home.

While hiding away upstairs I heard my mum call Cliff into the kitchen and shut the door. I think she understood how lost he was. I couldn't hear what they were saying but heard the sound of muffled sobs and could picture Mum putting her arms around Cliff and doing what she does best; being a mum who cares. I knew he had been holding in a lot of his emotions as he was too worried to let me see. I was so grateful to my mum at that moment.

As everyone was leaving later that afternoon my dad held back. He waited for it to be just the two of us and hugged me so hard I'm sure he was trying to hug the baby inside me.

"Whatever you want to do you know we'll be there. Whatever you decide, you do what you think is best. No matter what, we love you and we will love that baby. No matter what." His usually deep, gruff voice cracked, and he walked away.

After everyone left, Cliff and I didn't really talk. Not about what we might 'do' about the pregnancy. We were both waiting for the other one to start the conversation, scared of being honest in case the other didn't feel the same way. Cliff wanted more information, needed to know all the options. I was in denial I think. So again, we just waited.

The next day we had to go back to see the bereavement midwife. Looking over the paperwork she let slip the baby was a boy. We hadn't known this until that moment. We both looked at each other and she realised her mistake.

She carried on talking. Mainly about termination and what this would involve. It was clear the expectation was we would terminate; it was an assumed, unspoken agreement. We were then told we could, if we wanted to, see a consultant who could give us some more information on what Down syndrome meant and we gladly accepted this chance.

Big mistake.

Having sat in another waiting area we were shown into the apparently highly regarded consultant's room. A strong set man in a white coat who held himself with great authority and the bedside manner of a block of ice. He looked at our notes and explained to us in a really patronising manner that is was unlikely our baby would be able to live independently. He told us he would be unlikely to speak properly, would not go to mainstream school, may never be toilet trained and would need a lot of care and attention. That we were to expect to look after him for the rest of our lives.

We left the office in shock.

After checking back in with the rosy-cheeked midwife we were sent home and '*given some time to think about our options*'.

We were to let them know what we wanted to do.

Back home we both commented on the awful consultant and how he really needed a lesson in bedside manners. We were still skirting around the issue though. Neither of us ever really saying what we wanted.

At one point Cliff, raising his dark eyebrows, said: "Why us?"

My no-hesitation answer was: "Why not?"

As is often my way, I wrote down how I was feeling. In a letter to my oldest school friend who lived in Australia (this was in the days before emails) I poured out my heart.

Termination was not what I wanted, I wrote. I was scared of the procedure; the midwife had told me it would be like a short labour. But, more importantly, this was already my *baby*, I had already connected with him. We had produced him and he was part of me. I wrote I was worried about what Cliff really felt. I was scared to push him into something he wasn't comfortable with.

After I'd written the letter, in tears, I realised I had to tell Cliff how I was feeling. I think he was waiting for me to make the first move as he was hovering near me constantly.

"I know what I want to do," I said, almost to myself.

We sat down in our little conservatory we'd had built the year before and he listened to me talk, about my feelings for the baby, my worries, my fears. He comforted me, let me cry, let me rant and then with a vivid amount of relief said he completely agreed.

"This is *our* baby and no matter what, if he is strong enough to survive we are strong enough to cope."

Cliff said he too had been worrying about pushing me into a decision I wasn't sure about.

"When I asked earlier 'why us?' your answer was so honest and so obvious it has really made him think about things in a more positive light and I agree. Why not us?" he said, running his hands through his short, thick hair.

"We can – and will – deal with this you know," I said – I was assuring myself as much as him.

"Honestly, this is the first positive thing I've felt for weeks," Cliff said, staring at me earnestly whilst rubbing his hand over his dark stubble. He clearly felt as relieved as I did.

As soon as we had decided, as clichéd as it sounds, it felt like a weight had been lifted. We phoned the hospital and made an appointment to see the rosy-cheeked midwife to tell her our decision.

That's when the fun began ...

CHAPTER 3

SHARING THE GOOD NEWS

After nearly three weeks of waiting for the result, we were relieved to have answers at last. Most close friends and family were waiting to hear so there were many phone calls to make and take. Each one similar to the next.

A typical phone call would go something like this:

"We've had the results from the CVS. It proved positive. No, a positive result means the baby definitely does have Down syndrome. No, it's very unlikely to be wrong. Yes, we're sure. Yes, we are going ahead with the pregnancy. We're fine yes, obviously getting our heads around it and trying to stay positive."

The reactions varied, mostly supportive, some a bit odd, but mostly supportive. Often it felt people were really not sure how to react – whether to be happy or sad for us. I don't think we knew ourselves really. I found being positive myself helped. Friends who had never before shown such a compassionate side to their nature told me they loved me and offered touching words of support. I received heartfelt letters and notes from people to whom previously I had barely spoken.

The wife of one of my closer cousins – a very warm, spiritual lady – wrote to me about a young girl with Down syndrome whom she had recently met at a party and described how her smile lit up the room and her happy spirit was infectious. Another distant friend of Cliff's brothers who we hadn't seen in years, sent a beautiful card saying she was sure our new baby would prove challenging but wasn't it true all children can be and to ask for help if we needed it. Simple things like that went a long way.

Many friends and family assured us *'we would cope'* and while I always agreed, deep down I wondered how they could possibly know this. Some (who clearly didn't know us very well) said this wouldn't have happened to us if God didn't think we could handle it and suggested we had been blessed with this gift.

Seriously? I doubted any higher person would have looked at me and said: "Ooh let's make her mum of a child with extra needs she knows nothing about."

Others quite honestly said they thought we were brave and they admired our decision. Again, I wasn't sure I agreed, I didn't feel brave. Cliff and I were just doing what we felt was right for us and our family.

We did appreciate all of the support we received though, in whatever form. For us it was – and has always been – about acknowledgement. Nobody questioned if it was the right decision. An elderly family member tried to reassure us by saying the doctors didn't know everything and were probably wrong anyway. We didn't have the strength, or the inclination, to explain how accurate the tests were. She didn't mean anything by it, she was just trying to make us feel better. But, we didn't want to be made to feel better. We just wanted to get on with it.

I grieved. As did Cliff, and I guess our extended family. I grieved for the child I wasn't going to have, the 'normal' child I was expecting who wasn't to be. For the loss of the perfect baby I'd imagined. Not that he wasn't going to be perfect to us – just not in society's eyes. I also probably grieved for me, the life that was about to change in ways I had no idea about. Sometimes I'd cry randomly in the middle of the day, sometimes I'd just want to be alone and quiet. I don't remember us sharing our grief as it were. It wasn't that we would cry in bed together at night or spend hours discussing our decision. Again, we just wanted to get on with it.

Sam was two and a half and although he may not have understood what was going on I'm sure he picked up on the emotions we were dealing with.

We decided to tell him as best we could as soon as we found out. We explained his new brother would be born with Down syndrome and this *may* mean he would find things harder to do. We explained he may learn to sit up, walk, talk and so on, later than other babies and he would more than likely need extra help – we tried to focus on the positive. Sam accepted everything we told him and didn't seem overly concerned. At that age why would he be? It was more about getting him used to the term Down syndrome and preparing him for the fact his new brother was probably going to take up a lot of our time.

At that age Sam was a typical toddler, he loved playing with his cars, going to the park, had to have a ball near him at all times and was happily going to playschool. He had a love for dressing up and dancing that continued for years and was a fun kid to be around – if a bit noisy. From a young age, he'd turn the music up if a song came on he liked and dance around, often with me joining in. Anything from the latest pop song to a nursery rhyme, music was in his blood, Cliff – who used to DJ – would say.

My way of coping with anything I'm not sure about or that is worrying me is to get information. So, I tried to find out as much as I could about Down syndrome. I joined the Down Syndrome Association who sent through a whole pack of information, mostly very difficult to read at the time, but it gave us a valuable insight.

I got in touch with another mum who had a child with Down syndrome and on her invite, went along to another mum's house one day and joined in a coffee morning. A bit bizarre really as there I was pregnant and full of questions. There they were – a room full of babies and toddlers with Down syndrome.

I wasn't upset when I saw them, or shocked, or surprised – all emotions I'd prepared myself for before I went. I just drank it all in and asked questions. There were probably around five or six mums with their children and they were all friendly enough. I was in an unusual situation it seemed, as I already knew my baby had Down syndrome. All the other mums there had only found out after their children were born. Some were still quite clearly shocked by the situation and to be honest, some were bitter about it. I can only assume they felt cheated and were still coming to terms with the news. All totally understandable emotions and it actually made me grateful I had some time to adjust to the news before the baby arrived and I was knee deep in new baby fug. I remember there were a couple of women who were very upfront about the challenges they were facing. Questioning why the system isn't better set up to give the news in a more positive, kind and sensitive way.

They were fighting already.

That day and ever since, whenever I've met a parent of a child with Down syndrome, inevitably the talk turns to when and how they found out. A similar kind of story is told. Parents are told in a shockingly insensitive way. We are talking about the early

2000s, not the 1900s, and really it is quite unbelievable how badly the situation was – and still is – handled. For me being told by a secretary over the phone was pretty harsh, for others they found out when a nurse gasped and said, "Oh no he has Down syndrome", or doctors who have expressed their deep sympathy and dismay while conveying the news to medical staff, whispering by bedsides and shaking of heads. I have yet to meet – or in fact, hear about – one single person who was given the news in a positive way.

Okay, so it may not be news most people expect new parents to necessary celebrate, but if it was told in a more positive way, it would make such a difference to how parents go on to accept and bond with their child. Also offering parents some kind of counselling to help them come to terms with what they are being told should, in my opinion, be offered as standard. After all, it was made very clear to me I would have been given a lot more help and support had I decided not to keep my baby.

This and the issues surrounding how results are given are really a bugbear of many families I know.

Over the next few months, we had more scans to attend, mainly at King's College Hospital in London. They were to check the baby's heart, gut and other such stuff they could look for. Each one was stressful and every time we'd go along with a lot of trepidation; waiting for bad news. But, one by one, each scan ruled out serious heart issues, stomach problems and kidney complaints. We were beginning to feel positive that, despite the initial prognosis and the many issues we had been warned could come up, our son was actually going to be a healthy baby without any need for immediate surgery or having to stay in hospital for the first few weeks, or even months of his life.

After our third scan at King's, we were discharged and advised to go back to the consultant at the local hospital and carry on with the pregnancy as normal. Sadly, my consultant was the same arrogant, cold man we'd been to see before.

"I hope he's a little more positive this time," I whispered to Cliff as we waited in the local hospital for our appointment.

Having been shown in to his office he made a show of looking at my notes and then told us, quite bluntly, to ignore most of what we had been told at the scans so far. Apparently (in his opinion), any problems would not necessarily show up anyway, and certainly not before twenty-six weeks. It wasn't so much what he said (that was bad enough), but how he said it. Matter of factly, without considering our feelings at all. After starting to relax, and at last get ourselves emotionally prepared for our new arrival, we felt we were back to square one. Not knowing, worrying about the baby's health and in fear of major complications. The consultant may as well have slapped us in the face.

Bastard! I never went back to that particular consultant after then.

So, we could only wait for the baby to arrive to finally believe he was going to be okay.

Hello world!

Jamie arrived kicking and weeing after being delivered by caesarean section on 27 November 2000 weighing 2.76kg, three days earlier than planned and two weeks before his due date. Although any major heart issues had pretty much been ruled out, it was decided just in case there were any problems – and due to the fact that I'd had a difficult birth with Sam that led to an emergency caesarean – it would be better all-round if I had the baby by planned caesarean. But, a few days before

I was due to go into hospital I woke late one Sunday night with contractions. Nothing too strong, but as they began to become more frequent I thought: *"Shit, I'd forgotten how bad these are"* and then *"Shit, we need to get to hospital fast."*

We arrived at the hospital in the early hours of the morning and I was told I would go into surgery as soon as possible later that day. As they wheeled me down I was quite relaxed and Cliff, all dressed up in his hospital greens and cap, seemed relaxed too.

"It feels much easier than when we were here last. That was more like a scene from ER, do you remember?" he laughed at his own joke.

The mood was light, and we were both eager to meet our new son.

The operating room was a little tenser, but still nervous excitement was the main vibe. The midwife and the rest of the medical staff had been prepped and knew the baby had Down syndrome and so extra precautions had been put in place. Breathing equipment was ready on standby should he need it, and if necessary he could be whisked off to the Intensive Care Unit. I felt better for that, knowing we were actually in safe hands if we needed to be.

"You know we are aware our baby has Down syndrome, right?" I asked as a member of the medical team helped me in to position for the epidural.

"Yes, we're all aware," he replied and glanced at the nurse opposite.

I didn't want any negativity around us when he was born or any whispering behind hands or doubts about his condition. I wanted everyone to be ready for him in a positive and caring way. Still, there was a hushed tension in the room.

The delivery itself was straightforward. For anyone who's had a C-section you'll know it's the strangest feeling in the world. Exactly like it's described to you; it feels like someone is rummaging around in a bag that is resting on your stomach. The surgeon was very communicative and kept us up to date with what was happening. I think we were just all waiting for that beautiful noise when a baby is born – a wail yes, but a beautiful wail.

My immediate feeling when he was handed to me and I cradled him against me, once I could see him living and breathing, was relief.

He was alive, he was here, and he was ours!

"Wow! He's got ginger hair!" Cliff said laughing.

"Bloody hell, as if he hasn't got enough to contend with, he's going to be ginger as well!" I said flippantly, grinning and high on the euphoria of finally meeting him.

Everyone laughed and the tension in the room eased. It wasn't until later, after Jamie had been cleaned up and his blonde hair revealed, I was reminded of this and joked with Cliff how he'd told the whole family he had ginger hair.

While in hospital, we were given a private side room – *'free of charge under the circumstances'.* This was fine by me, as I didn't want to be on the ward. Not because I was hiding away, I just liked my privacy. I'd chosen to pay for a private room when Sam was born for the same reason.

But it felt like the hospital was hiding us away. Maybe they thought it would upset the other new mums? Perhaps they thought I'd spend the whole time in floods of tears? I guess they were just trying to be helpful.

My parents were waiting for us when we came out of surgery and came to see us as soon as we'd settled into our room. Everyone responded with so much love and affection. Nobody gave us the impression they felt anything but the typical baby awe and excitement that surrounds the arrival of a baby in our family. Everyone wanted a cuddle, they all compared features and there was the usual *'who does he look like'* conversations.

Despite initially calling him Harry, we changed our minds after a few hours and settled on the name Jamie – a name Sam had suggested months before. Part of the reason for this was my dad's way of pronouncing 'Arry – we joked for years afterwards that his Essex accent was the reason J had been renamed.

Already comparisons were being made to Sam, although Jamie was much fairer than Sam was. He had a head of straight blonde hair with tufts sticking straight up at the back and was a healthy size.

He was perfect to us.

I would say everyone without fail seemed to hold Jamie a little bit more delicately and with slightly more care than I'd seen before. As if he were more fragile I guess. My mum and sisters especially seemed to hold him with a real sense of fierce protection; they had his back from the start.

When Sam met him, it was particularly special of course. Becoming a big brother was something he'd been looking forward to and he was excited he had finally arrived.

As I'd got my bags ready to go in to hospital to have Jamie – following all the usual bits of advice about making sure the older sibling doesn't feel left out at all – I'd snuck a little present in the hospital bag ready for when Sam first met his new brother. Sam had also bought Jamie a special gift – a Dalmatian dog similar to one he had loved as a baby. He had recorded a special message for his new brother which could be heard when you squeezed its paw. When Sam met Jamie for the first time he kept pressing its paw to play it over and over to him. This exchanging of presents was the start of a pretty strong bond between them and there was no drama, no jealous outbursts.

"Was I little like Jaymee?" Sam asked, already making Jamie's name sound right.

"Did I make that noise? Why does he keep falling asleep? Can I give him his toy?" Sam was his usual inquisitive self. He was eager to hold him and bored with the baby talk very quickly. All very normal and refreshing.

"He looks like you when you were born Sam," I told him, and he glowed with pride.

They did look similar to me, despite the different hair colouring, I could see the family bond. Jokes were already being made about Dad's chin.

Over the next couple of days various midwives were sent to visit us to look at Jamie and his 'pointers'. These pointers are the specific features associated with Down syndrome.

The deep crease across the palm – *possibly*;

the gap between the first and second toe – *no he didn't have that*;

the ears being low down – *er, maybe*;

and of course, the hypotonia – *a posh word for floppiness*.

As each nurse, midwife and doctor looked over Jamie I would watch them pick him up and then lay him back down, ticking off each one – mentally and literally on their clipboards.

At times it felt as if we were a side show. Strange as it sounds though, I didn't object. I knew it was important the midwives in particular saw Jamie as a newborn baby. I knew it would help them to learn first-hand what to look out for should they suspect Down syndrome in newborns. Many of these professionals had never even seen a newborn with confirmed Down syndrome. In hindsight, I hope my lack of negativity rubbed off on them and most importantly they would learn how to react to other mums in my position.

Visits from various trainee paediatricians, doctors and so on, were slightly more galling. All of them would lay Jamie down and lift his leg or arm and then watch it flop down, nodding their heads knowingly as they did so.

It got to a stage where I didn't need to wait for their questions, I began showing them which pointers he had and which he didn't so much.

"Can you see how his big toe is slightly further from his second toe, but not much. You can see the crease on his palm though," I would say. That way the visits were over quicker.

SCREENING FOR DOWN SYNDROME AFTER BIRTH

If you did not know your baby had Down syndrome pre-birth the most common way it is diagnosed after birth is through a blood test. The test will check the number of chromosomes your baby has. Those with Down syndrome have an extra 21st chromosome.

The blood test will likely be taken after your doctor, midwife or nurse have checked for signs I talk about above, such as low muscle tone. However, not all babies with Down syndrome present with all of these signs. If you are unsure ask to speak to someone or contact the Down Syndrome Association or equivalent in your country.

My advice is to get help and support early. Tell people you feel comfortable with and allow yourself as much time as you need to digest, understand, grieve and accept your child's diagnosis.

(www.downs-syndrome.org.uk/for-new-parents)

There is a fantastic video made by children with Down syndrome explaining how Trisomy 21 occurs. It's made by Shabang Inclusive Learning.

(www.youtube.com/watch?v=o0VV3C_ydak)

Not such a healthy start

We were allowed home after a few days, only to have to go back in to hospital the following day when Jamie developed diarrhoea. He spent the night in an incubator with me sleeping on a put-you-up bed next to it. After some failed attempts at latching on it was decided that introducing bottles would be a good idea and he was allowed home once again after he managed to keep some milk down and his bowels were deemed okay.

Being sick was an issue from the start, which was a huge surprise to me as Sam had never been a baby that was sick after feeding. But Jamie did and continued to be. He was also very 'snuffly' as if he had a constant heavy cold. This would be far worse at night-time and was quite worrying as we often heard him coughing and spluttering. So much so that sometimes, in those first few months, on our health visitor's advice we took to letting him sleep in his car seat as it meant he was more upright.

After one particularly awful night we called an ambulance as we were woken to the sound of him choking. We were taken in to the children's ward and the hospital did their best to help him clear his mucus and sent us home.

It was a few weeks later that we were sent back to the hospital by our local GP as he was concerned Jamie was still quite congested. It was then we found out Jamie actually had bronchiolitis. According to the paediatrician we saw, this was quite common in babies at that time of year. After monitoring him for a few hours, again they cleared his airways by sucking away some of the mucus and sent us home with an inhaler and told us to carry on doing what we were doing. Which basically meant getting up half a dozen times a night to sit him up, bang him on the back and help him clear the phlegm. We soon learnt that the congestion was something we would need to learn to live with as every winter would bring about a cold that led to lots of mucus.

In those early days, I thought a lot about what people saw when they looked at him. Whether the fact he had Down syndrome was obvious. Nobody ever said anything. When we were out, I would think I'd notice people taking a second look and would challenge their stares. In hindsight, I can see it was me with the issue; they were just admiring the baby the way everyone does with a newborn.

I expressed this feeling once to a friend and she rather bluntly told me of course you could tell he had Down syndrome, it was like asking if you could tell a black man was black! I think she was trying to be helpful?

After the terrible meeting with the consultant and the constant negativity we'd felt from many of the medical people we'd been in contact with during the pregnancy, I didn't hold out much hope when we were due to attend our first appointment with Jamie's allocated paediatrician. However, Doctor Puvanendran turned out to be completely different to all the doctors we'd met so far. He was a very forward-thinking man and the first medical person we met who was positive from the start. He was almost spiritual in his attitude – not religious, it was more about his whole attitude. He told us with the right support and input our son could lead a fulfilling life.

During our appointment, I explained Jamie fed well, was mainly being bottle fed (I was still trying to feed him myself, but he never latched on for very long), but that he was constantly sick and had been very congested.

"I don't mean he's a little bit sick either. He is sick A LOT!" I gestured with my hands to emphasise my point.

He assured me this would settle down but to let him know if it didn't. The rest of the appointment he encouraged us to think positively about Jamie's development and told us about Targeted Nutritional Intervention. He explained nutritional supplements were thought to be of great benefit and in other countries it was being suggested to parents early on. He gave us details of a man called Peter Elliot who founded the Down Syndrome Research Foundation (DSRF) and who was a key spokesperson for nutritional intervention.

After the appointment both Cliff and I were intrigued, and I called Peter that day and left a message. I was surprised when he called me back the following day and we spent over an hour talking on the phone. He told me that when his son David was born some twenty years earlier, he and his wife were also led to believe he wouldn't achieve very much but they ignored all the experts and fought long and hard to help him become as fit, active and able as he could be. Peter became somewhat of an expert on Down syndrome, and through research found out about nutritional intervention. In 1996, he set up the DSRF charity to inform other parents and to raise awareness as well as advocate for the need for more research. He advised me what supplements I could take while breastfeeding and what the recommendations were for babies.

There was a lot of stuff I didn't understand about antioxidants, good fats and bad fats, vitamins, minerals and so on. I wrote as I listened, taking in as much information as I could. I then passed the information on to Cliff who looked it all up on the internet at work – at that time, we didn't have access to the internet at home. It was probably then we decided the internet was a necessity at home and shortly after got ourselves online.

There began a long, love-hate relationship with the wonders of the internet.

TARGETED NUTRITIONAL INTERVENTION

Not widely used in the UK, Targeted Nutritional Intervention (TNI) is a specific nutritional supplement program that has been designed to address the metabolic disturbances in Down syndrome. There are six basic products that are slowly introduced to the individual with Down syndrome, one at a time. Each of these components has a specific role in diminishing the negative effects of the known metabolic disturbances in Down syndrome. In-depth information on the resulting benefits can be found on the TNI Research page.

It is a mixture of vitamins, minerals, amino acids, fatty acids and digestive enzymes targeted to reduce the biological impacts of that extra 21st chromosome.

(www.trisomy21research.org/2017/04/25/using-tni-a-beginners-guide/ and
www.facebook.com/groups/1402961166638701)

CHAPTER 4

MAKING PROGRESS

As we settled into our new family life there were appointments to keep and developments to track. I had ordered the 'Children with Down syndrome' pages from the DSA to insert in to his 'red book' (the Personal Child Health Record Book, PCHR) that contained a list of the basic minimum health checks for babies with Down syndrome. Much more realistic than the standard one given to parents and it helped to avoid lots of worry. At Jamie's eight-week check he would have been recorded as failing most of his milestones, but thanks to the PCHR charts, I knew he was on track.

His communication was coming on leaps and bounds – this was the thing I had homed in on most. For me, speech – or communication – was the key to many things. He was smiling, rolling and chuckling by five months. We spent a lot of time singing with Jamie, using actions and encouraging any kind of response. Even if he just smiled or pointed towards something he wanted, we would whoop and clap so he knew he was being understood.

Sam came along to physiotherapy appointments with us when Jamie was a baby. He would join in sliding down the slides to show Jamie how it was done, helping him to balance by holding his arms or legs and jumping in to the ball pit with him to stop him crying.

"Come on JJ [Sam called him this from when he was a baby and it stuck], you can do it!" Sam would shout while zipping down the slide.

Jamie would always chuckle at his brother and more often than not his encouragement worked. For the more mundane stuff like doctor's appointments, Sam happily stayed with Nanna. He seemed to enjoy being big brother and was quick to pick up on things we were doing to help Jamie. He was there when, at six months old, Jamie rolled over for the first time. Sam was sitting to the side of Jamie who was lying on his mat and encouraging him with his favourite toy. He was so pleased when Jamie finally tipped over rather unsteadily from back to front and continued to play this 'game' with him for weeks after. He would help him sit up by making sure he was surrounded by a buffer of pillows and gently propping him back up when he invariably wobbled over.

One day, when Jamie was very young, we were sitting at the dinner table and out of the blue, Sam asked me why he didn't have Down syndrome.

"Will I get it when I'm older? Will Jamie always have it?" he asked, his brown eyes wide with real interest.

He said it in such a matter-of-fact way that it made it easier for me to answer without getting emotional.

I explained it as best I could.

"No, you won't ever get it as you have to be born with it. Some babies are born with it, most are not. Jamie was and so will always have Down syndrome, it's not ever going to go away, but that's okay."

Sam took in what I said, and the conversation was over quite quickly. I didn't mention chromosomes and genetics. He didn't ask any more questions.

But it played on my mind afterwards. What made him ask I wondered? Did I say the right things? Did I give the right answers? Should I have said more?

After that, while we had the odd conversation about what having Down syndrome meant, that was the one and only time Sam really questioned me.

I learned Signalong – a sign language developed for children with communication issues – from when Jamie was around six months old. I went along to classes that were being run by our then speech therapist. Once a week for an hour I would sit in a room at our local health centre with half a dozen other mums whose children also had communication issues and learn signs like 'milk' or 'thank you'. We all had our babies with us and between us we'd muddle through the session trying to learn the signs whilst attending to the demands of our children. It was hectic but good fun. When I got home, I was eager to practise and Sam immediately wanted to learn it too so I taught him words and signs and we'd use them throughout the week. By this time my friend Nic had had another baby – a boy called Ted – and we'd often meet up with them (with her daughter Isobel) and Samantha and her girls (April and Beckie) and practise our signs with them too.

New friends

By ten months Jamie was sitting on his own. At eleven months, he pulled himself up on the furniture, and although walking still proved elusive, we were now having regular physiotherapy appointments that were really paying off. It was around this time we met a lady called Karen and her beautiful daughter Holly who was born just two weeks after Jamie in the same hospital. It took our amazing physiotherapist Deana to get us together. We both questioned afterwards why the midwives, nurses at the hospital, or even the health visitor we both saw hadn't thought to tell us about each other.

I liked Karen immediately, she was straight talking, no nonsense and a fighter. I realised within the first half hour of our meeting up for a cup of tea at my house. Holly was poorly for the first couple of weeks and had had a small hole in her heart, but apart from that she and Jamie were similar in their development. Karen was always trying new things – I'll never forget going around to their house and seeing an empty box of washing powder attached to the front legs of Holly's chair. To help her sit properly, apparently.

Jamie, Holly, and another little girl, Ellie, were invited to join a fantastic little group run by one of the most open and caring women we were fortunate to meet in Jamie's early years. Jane Hill ran the developmental playgroup at our local community hospital and once a week we would go along there. Jane had an older son who had special needs and she was always encouraging us to push for more help, ask for more services and gave lots of good, sensible advice. During the group Jamie would clap along to the songs, throw the ball, play with the foam and generally have a great time. We looked forward to this every week.

Jamie continued to make steady progress and his speech was really coming on. He said his first word 'Dadda' at around seven months and followed it by 'Mumma' a couple of months later. Frustratingly for me he then stopped saying 'Mumma' and instead used a variation of 'Dadda' *('aahdee')* for a long while. We could all tell the difference as his intonation changed, but he lost the 'mm' sound. Again, this was something we would later learn happens. He would learn something. Then forget it, then re-learn again.

He loved to hear the sound of his own voice though – as did I – and we woke most mornings to the sound of babbling from his cot. He also began to feed himself finger food (I had started weaning him at five months) and despite having quite a severe reaction to any fruit he ate – his face and the top of his head would go bright red – he ate well. He'd also started taking the TNI supplement and despite a second bout of bronchiolitis, was doing well.

Since I had spoken to Peter Elliot, I had become actively involved with the Down Syndrome Research Foundation. Via the website I got in touch with other parents who I immediately felt I could relate to and we talked via a forum on the website. They too didn't want their children to be victims, they wanted them to be an active part of society. They didn't want to roll over and accept their fate, they felt they had a hand to play in it. It was a relief to hear such positive attitudes from other people; and to hear such good news about how much their children had achieved, despite what the parents had been told. I continued to learn what I could and to talk to other parents.

However, while the DSRF and other charities were invaluable, informative, insightful and a lifeline, they were also my undoing in some ways.

There was so much information, so many ways to help Jamie's development, so many things to look into it became overwhelming. I would spend hours looking up therapies and wading through medical information, unable to make head nor tail of most of it. Each week there was something else to help Jamie fulfil his potential. A way of getting him to respond, move and communicate – and each one I was scared to let pass. I didn't want to fail Jamie. It wasn't that I was looking for a way to cure him as such – or at least I don't think that's what I was looking to do. I was just constantly inspired and amazed by how children like Jamie could develop and what they could achieve – with the right help.

I didn't realise how much pressure I was putting on myself – and probably the rest of the family – until one particular night when Jamie was around two years old.

The Daffodil Principle

Sam, who had started at our local village school when Jamie was two and he was a month off five years old, had begun to show he was aware, and maybe a little jealous, of the extra attention Jamie got. Just the time spent going to appointments and caring for Jamie meant Sam would often have to wait for my attention. So, we were making lots of effort to make sure he got special time with each of us too. As a result, I'd offered to go along to his first school disco as a parent helper (this was at that lovely age when your mum being at the school disco wasn't embarrassing!). I was tasked with keeping an eye on the children in the main hall as they skidded around, filled themselves up on sugar and generally had a ball. Seeing Sam with all his friends was great and he had a fantastic night. On the way home he was chatting nonstop and couldn't wait to tell his dad all about it.

After we got home and after Sam had gone to bed I sat down at the kitchen table and out of the blue completely broke down.

'Would Jamie ever go to a school disco? Would he have friends to run about with? Would he even be able to run? Will he be allowed to go the local school too? If not, where would he go?'

All of these thoughts and fears came tumbling out. Cliff, who had been at home looking after Jamie obviously had no idea what was going on and didn't know what to say or do. I tried to tell him but really couldn't understand it myself. He tried to comfort me and reassure me but was also completely bewildered by my outburst. I eventually stopped crying and went to bed, dismissing the whole episode as my just being hormonal.

Over the next few weeks I couldn't shift the black cloud that had descended over me. I felt unsure of myself and found I was worrying more about Jamie's development and making sure he was being encouraged enough. My friend Nic spotted I was struggling and during a chat suggested I try reiki. Her friend had recently tried it and she said she had heard good things about it through other people too.

"What harm would it do Jo?" she said.

To be honest, at that point I knew I needed something and was willing to give anything a go. So I got the number from Nic's friend and booked myself an appointment for the following week,

Reiki, a Japanese healing technique and form of alternative medicine, is used to relieve stress and promote relaxation. It's a very strange thing to experience and even harder to explain.

The therapist – a reiki master – channels energy into you by means of touch to activate natural healing and help restore emotional well-being. After a reiki session you, as the patient, are meant to feel more balanced and rested.

I went along on the appointed evening and after a very lengthy session of reiki, although I didn't feel immediately 'better' I did feel very relaxed. I chatted to the reiki master about what had brought me to her. I explained about Jamie and that I felt this need to find out all I could as soon I could in case I missed anything that could help him. I worried I wasn't doing enough to help him. She listened to me and then gave me a copy of a story about a woman in America who grew daffodils, *The Daffodil Principle**.

The story was about a beautiful field of daffodils one woman had created next to her house. It was so amazing people come from all over the country to see it. By the side of her house she had put up a sign saying:

The answers to the questions I know you are asking:
50,000 bulbs
One at a time
By one woman
2 hands, 2 feet and very little brain
Began in 1958

It talked about one woman in particular who visited the daffodil field with her daughter. The woman became sad for the things she herself could have achieved had she just got on with it – one day at a time, little by little. Her daughter had to remind her what the Daffodil Principle really was about. Simply by saying "start tomorrow".

It took me a while to understand why the reiki master felt the need to pass this story on to me. But over the next few days it clicked. I was trying to do too much, too quickly. Expecting results too soon. I was becoming overwhelmed by the possibilities and often didn't know where to start. I needed to remember it may take a long time to get there but going steadily, one step at a time was the best way.

I decided to make a conscious effort to take a step back. I needed to stop worrying I was going to miss something important, be fussier with what I was learning, and stop panicking I was missing the boat with some stuff.

I had to remind myself it would all still be there tomorrow. I could plant that bulb then. For now, the bulbs I had planted needed nurturing. That was enough.

The Daffodil Principle by Jaroldeen Asplund Edwards

SIGNALONG

Signalong is a key word sign-supported communication system based on British sign language and is used in spoken word order. Founded in the UK, it uses speech, sign, body language, facial expression and voice tone to reference the link between sign and word.

Using sign language as well as words can help children develop language by giving them other tools to use when actual language production is hard. It gives them confidence in their communication and reduces frustration. Other systems such as Makaton are also used and you may want to check with your local speech therapist which system your local authority suggests.

(www.signalong.org.uk)

CHAPTER 5

PLAYSCHOOL

Jamie was just eight months old when we had our first visit from an educational psychologist (EP). I thought at the time, *what the hell could education have to do with my baby?* But accepted the appointment with optimism and curiosity.

She was a nice enough lady who asked lots of questions and assessed Jamie and us in a roundabout way. One of her first questions – or statements really – was: "Jamie will go to mainstream school, yes?"

At the time, his schooling wasn't even on our radar really. While we had vaguely thought about it, we hadn't really gone into any detail. But, when she explained he would be given support, I agreed yes, mainstream would be our preferred choice. At the time, I was still naive about many things – schooling being one of them. I was happy to hear, and believe that Jamie would receive all the support he needed in whatever setting we chose.

As he got older we saw various EPs (they changed like the wind, almost as often as his speech therapists), and their job was to ensure Jamie's needs were being met once he started by liaising with playschool, and later on, school. Before then, it was to assess him to see if he needed a statement of educational needs and help us find the right setting for him.

We started looking seriously at options for playschools after his second birthday. He had just started walking around this time – although it took him a few more months to gain enough confidence to let go of our hands and walk on his own – but he was becoming stronger and steadier on his feet each day.

My mum, who was always crawling around on all fours with Jamie encouraging him to walk loves to say it was the 'balloon trick' that got him going. She had – with all her grandchildren – used a balloon to entice them in to walking, with Dad clapping on the sidelines and ready to jump should anyone fall. Her 'trick' was to take their minds off the fact they were standing on their own two feet by holding the balloon just ahead of their reach. Like the proverbial carrot I guess.

With speech therapy and us encouraging his signing, his communication was really coming on too and he loved to have 'conversations' with us. Although there weren't many words as such, the expression, intonation and signing combined meant we could figure out what he was saying – but it took patience and a good ear. Overall, I was confident he was ready to take this next step and start playschool, but it was a question of where. We'd been advised by our EP to look at a variety of playgroups, including nurseries that catered for children with special needs.

We were particularly interested to hear that a new nursery was being set up in a large special needs school not far away from where we were living. It seemed the nursery, whose staff were trained in the development of children with special needs, could provide the care Jamie needed. He was still in nappies during the day and they didn't bat an eyelid when I called to talk to them and mentioned this – something that did worry me a lot.

However, when we informed the EP we would like to consider putting Jamie's name down for this particular nursery we were told he couldn't go there. According to the local authority, his needs weren't the *'right kind'* for this particular nursery. They never really explained what this meant. The only assumption we could make was it was because Jamie wasn't diagnosed with autism. At the time, the nursery was being set up as a nursery for children on the autistic spectrum. I didn't wish to take away from those children, but I did wonder why there wasn't a nursery geared up for Down syndrome if that was the case. So, we continued to look elsewhere.

Another special needs school a little further from us also had designated places for younger children. We went along to this school for a visit, but it was clear from the start this was a very different ball game. Many of the children there were severely disabled both mentally and physically, and the amount of care and attention they needed was way beyond what Jamie needed. We didn't feel that setting was right for Jamie.

In the end, we opted to send Jamie to our local village playgroup. Sam had gone there, and they knew us fairly well and, as we hoped Jamie would go on to the local school, it made sense. It was a traditional type of playschool where kids were allowed to play, get messy, run around and have fun. As playschool, in my opinion, *should* be about playing and learning to socialise, we were happy with our decision. But, we were also aware of the need to prepare him for the structure and expectations of school, so we also found a private day nursery where, we were told, he would be given one-to-one support. Two months before his third birthday he began two mornings a week at the local playgroup and six weeks later two afternoons at the private nursery. Perfect!?

Jamie was very happy at the local playgroup. The staff and children alike adored him, and every morning would be there to greet him with a hug and a huge shriek of "Jaimeeeee!". His assigned worker was always very open and honest with us and Jamie felt safe there. He made friends with children who he could go on to start school with and they were trying to learn and introduce signs to the whole group. Jamie was by now obsessed with the television character Barney – a purple dinosaur that sang and danced – and he would watch videos featuring him over and over again. His favourite sign to use was *'Barney'* and every child in the playschool could sign *'Barney'* too. By this time, he was also signing *'please'*, *'thank you'*, *'yes'*, *'drink'*, amongst other signs. So, the playschool getting on board was a huge help.

But he did struggle. He was still in nappies and sometimes I felt this was an issue for some members of staff. There were times when I knew he was being babied and I felt they should be pushing him more. He was small in both height and build and this probably didn't help as he looked younger than his peers. He didn't get the amount of one-to-one support he needed to prepare him for moving on to school, mainly because the staff weren't trained and didn't necessarily know HOW to help him. Often, I would hear he didn't join in something and know it was because no one encouraged him or explained to him what was happening. But, they tried their best and it was a place he was happy to go to and was accepted for himself.

The private nursery however wasn't working out. He was never as happy to go there as he was to go to playschool and didn't appear to have any friends there. Quite abruptly, after just a few months, his one-to-one support told us she no longer wanted to work with him with no reason why. The nursery manager didn't offer us any alternatives and we felt this was a sign they were not quite as keen for Jamie to be there as they first made out.

From the start, I felt that wherever Jamie went, the people he was with or those who were working with him, had to WANT to work with him. Otherwise, I know he feels that negativity – and we as his parents certainly do. So, we stopped his place there and extended his mornings at playschool. Not ideal, but he was happier.

This was the start of learning to accept that sometimes we just had to settle for less.

Angels in disguise

Around this time two very special people came in to our lives. After speech therapy through the local health service was proving sporadic and unreliable we had decided to invest in private speech therapy. Through an internet search I found a lady who sounded like she had the right experience. Geraldine proved to be a godsend. A professional-looking woman, with perfectly tousled blonde hair, a beaming smile and always immaculately turned out, she arrived carrying her ever-present bag of tricks that included bubbles, books, games and toys and immediately tuned in to Jamie's way of thinking.

She knew she had to win him over through his love (now obsession) of Barney. She spent the first few weeks trying to persuade Jamie to switch off the television. The next few weeks persuading him to *play* with her, and after that things just clicked and we never looked back. It was clear she knew what she was doing and I'm sure that was the difference in Jamie's early communication. She was also our sounding board if we had any problems and I would also often ask her opinion on new ideas I was trying or therapies I'd read about.

Another person who was important to us then was a lady called Helena. Cliff's cousin – whose son has autism and attended a local special needs school – introduced us to her following a conversation we'd had about his lack of progress at playschool. While he was loving it, he was developing quite a cheeky streak. This meant he'd often choose to ignore the playschool aunties or pretend he couldn't understand things we knew he could.

"Oh, he does make us laugh when he pulls our tops and signs for more biscuits, he's so cute we just have to give in."

As a teacher of children with special needs, Helena was newly qualified when we first met her and she agreed to do some work teaching him some very basic, but essential things. Age-related skills like nursery rhymes, answering questions like *'How old are you?' and 'What's your name?'* She also helped him with counting, phonics and so on. When he stood in front of the television and screamed for it to be turned on, she would patiently say (and sign) he had to wait until after he'd done his work. Again, like Geraldine, she tuned in to him and knew when to push him and when to back off. She helped him to understand how to follow instructions, how to ask for things and generally helped us prepare him for starting school. She also knew about the sleeping problems and assured us many other parents she met had similar issues.

She advised on things like potty training, that had started in vengeance when Jamie was three-and-a-half. While the school she was working at used the ABA (Applied Behavioural Analysis) approach, I knew this wasn't for Jamie and she agreed, but she had some good advice on introducing a routine of going to the toilet and reward-based learning.

Her weekly visits became something I looked forward to as I knew it was a time I could get on and do something knowing Jamie was happy learning.

With this extra input from Geraldine and Helena on top of playschool, plus of course our constant reminders in speech, signing, following instructions, learning to take turns and so on, he was making slow but steady progress. Toilet training though was still proving to be a harder nut to crack. But we were beginning to get ready for him to start school.

SPEECH THERAPY AND COMMUNICATION

Speech therapy is an intervention service that focuses on improving a child's speech and their ability to understand and express language, including non-verbal language. A Speech Therapist (ST) or Speech and Language Pathologist (SLP) are the professionals who provide this service.

What is provided free of charge really varies from borough to borough in the UK. It is widely recognised and acknowledged that children with Down syndrome do benefit – and require – help in this area. Ask your health visitor to refer you if necessary.

According to the DSE, "It can be argued that speech and language therapy is the most important part of intervention services for children with Down syndrome if we wish to promote their cognitive (mental) and social development."

In my experience, Total Communication – using all forms of communication from body language, pictures, signing and expression as well as actual talking – was vital to Jamie's communication.

Some children with Down syndrome also have physiological problems that may affect their speech. Again, a speech therapist can help with this.

(www.library.down-syndrome.org/en-us/news-update/02/2/speech-language-therapy-down-syndrome)

Toilet humour

Many things have taken Jamie a bit longer to learn. Learning to use the toilet being one of them. I started thinking about toilet training when he was about three-and-a-half, but it was clear at that age he was nowhere near ready. His understanding of what we were asking him to do was just not there. With any child, there is no point trying until they are ready. With Jamie's lack of coordination, getting him to get to the toilet and pull down his trousers was hard enough – but getting him there before he did anything was even harder. His brain just didn't process the information quickly enough.

It was the April before he started school that I tried again. It wasn't that he'd shown signs of being 'ready' – I'd got to the stage when I honestly didn't think he was ever going to be ready. I was at this time pregnant with Louise so with another baby on the way I felt if I didn't tackle it soon, I never would. I was concerned he would start school in September and be in the playground one day and one of the other children say something like, "Miss, why is Jamie wearing a nappy?"

He was on half-term from playschool which meant that we could stay indoors as much as we needed – which we did. It was hard work. For that whole week, I had to constantly take him to the toilet every fifteen minutes. He knew and could use the sign for toilet but rarely asked to go. He wouldn't use a potty so instead I'd bought a child seat that attached to an ordinary toilet.

"Toilet?" I would sign and say every half an hour.

Shaking his blonde head, he would say "no" so adamantly his glasses would rattle (he'd started wearing glasses a few months before) and try to run away from me.

After catching him I would sit with him in the bathroom for what felt like hours.

Sam, ever the helpful brother would encourage him by asking if he needed to go and I'd hear shouts of, "Mum, quick, he's going!" and I'd rush in to the living room or wherever they were to catch it in the potty. But poor Sam soon got bored with it, especially as we were housebound.

Number twos was a whole other issue and for that we needed military-style surveillance.

"Yay, good boy Jamie, you did a poo on the toilet," I'd say with as much excitement as I could muster each time we got the timing right. Jamie would merrily clap along and cheer, waving his hands in the air, very pleased with himself.

"Dun poo-poo, Sa," he'd proudly state and Sam would roll his eyes but clap along too, trying his best to encourage him while probably wondering when the hell it would stop being such a big deal.

Slowly but surely things started to improve and within a couple of months we were all pleasantly surprised that the number of accidents had decreased. Enough so he was without nappies in the day.

Not out of the woods

But, as ever, that was not the end of it. For a long while I, and the rest of the family, were on what I can only describe as 'poo-watch'. At times, it felt like it had taken over our existence.

Jamie still very rarely asked to go the toilet. This meant taking him regularly and looking out for signs he may need to go. It may have been obvious to us he needed the toilet, but he would kick, scream and fight, rather than take that simple walk to the loo.

The new job of poo control led to some of the most embarrassing incidents involving Jamie, and some of the most upsetting. And, looking back now, also some of the funniest.

He had accidents at friends' houses, while we were out shopping, at the park, at the cinema watching films – you name it, he's been there. The ball pool at a child's birthday party was not great. Especially when, as I changed him in the toilet afterwards, I could hear a lady next door asking her daughter how her trousers had got so wet when she clearly hadn't had an accident herself. I cringed and stayed in the cubicle until she was gone. At the time, Jamie was fairly new to toilet training, so I tried not to feel too guilty or upset by it.

But, as the years passed it became more difficult to disguise the embarrassment we all felt. One particular time stands out – and always will – as one of the most embarrassing times. A point at which I felt I'd lost hope, patience, and the will to live!

Jamie had been invited to a boy's party from playschool, whose mum I didn't know that well, but Jamie talked about this boy so I knew they were friends. The party was held at a soft play centre near us. Although he was now at an age when he would have preferred to stay home and play on his PSP I'd encouraged Sam to come along. I knew Jamie quite liked it at this particular play centre, so I was confident they would both enjoy it. Not long into the party and I noticed a little damp patch on Jamie's trousers and took him to the bathroom. For some reason, I only had a few wipes in my bag and no spare clothes (I would usually carry lots, along with spare clothes) so I cleaned him up as best I could. I removed his damp pants and thought going commando wouldn't hurt for an hour or so.

Back out into the play area and he was off. A little while later, Sam came running over to me.

"Mum, I think Jamie needs a poo, he smells a bit," he whispered looking a bit sheepish.

Sam by then had a built-in sensor to Jamie's toilet habits (as we all did). I whipped Jamie into the loo and sure enough, he'd had a slight accident. Nothing too serious though, so again I cleaned him up and let him get on with it.

Big Mistake!

In the meantime, one of Sam's school friends had arrived with his little brother so Sam was really enjoying himself too. I was keeping an eye on Jamie who was off playing and I hoped that was the end of it. But soon after, a very embarrassed looking Sam came running over looking really anxious:

"Mum, quick! Mum, come on!" He pulled me towards the middle of the play area. "Jamie needs to go to the toilet now. Quick, Mum!"

As I saw Jamie I watched him lift his leg oddly, and I knew. Looking down on the floor, he put his leg back down and then walked off – stepping over the offending mess as carefully as he could. Thank goodness it wasn't a runny one!

Whether it was my shocked face, or the fact they had smelt the evidence, a couple of the other mums soon realised what was going on. As I picked Jamie up, they whisked their children away from the – actually very small – mess.

I desperately looked around for help, but no one seemed to see me. Not having anyone else to ask, I had to tell Sam to stand by the mess, while I ran to the mum whose son's party it was to get some wipes, grabbing Jamie by the arm on the way. I cleaned up the mess one-handed, while pinning Jamie down with the other hand. I could see how embarrassed Sam was and I was very flustered. Having cleaned up the floor I scooped Jamie up and, calling to Sam to get our stuff, cleaned him up as best I could in the bathroom. There wasn't much I could do about his trousers. I cursed myself for not having a spare pair of trousers as now Jamie would have to ride home in the car wearing nothing down below but a cloth muslin square I found at the bottom of the changing bag. Sam was waiting outside the bathroom door looking really awkward and I felt so awful for him. I didn't know what to say.

"Let's go, shall we?" I tried to give him a reassuring smile but he shrugged and we made a very swift exit.

Humiliated, upset, angry, sad. I – and I'm sure Sam – basically felt like the little mess Jamie had created.

It wasn't even Jamie I was most upset with – although I was bloody annoyed with him – it was the other parents there. Not one of them offered to help, no one made any attempt to help me feel less embarrassed and nobody tried to make the situation better. A simple: "bloody kids, drive you mad, don't they?" would have done. Or someone could have helped in some way.

Looking back, I can now see the funny side of that day. But it's taken a while.

We carried on having many poo incidents but I was always prepared for the worse. I tried not to stress about it and just see it as something we had to deal with. Sometimes Jamie couldn't be bothered to go to the toilet, other times he didn't get there on time and sometimes we were not always right there to take him.

I've had poo in my fingernails, on my clothes, on my face, on the walls – in fact, I became almost blasé about it. *Almost*.

But, hey, it is only poo. It could be worse.

CHAPTER 6

CHOOSING SCHOOLS – MAINSTREAM OR NOT?

When Jamie turned four we had to start thinking about where it was he might go to school. The local mainstream school was at the top of our list of where *we'd* like him to go but felt we should look at all the options. We requested visits to two special needs schools – one in our local catchment area and one outside, both of which we had heard good reports about. While the education department said it was *our* choice, there was always an underlying feeling this wasn't actually the case.

After visiting the special needs school in our catchment area, we were told it was very unlikely there would be any places for him as it had long waiting lists. The school outside our local area also appealed to us, and had spaces, but the local authority made it clear they wouldn't be able to fund transport. This was frustrating, but we had to be practical. With Cliff now working for a new company he was travelling a lot, so the school run was down to me. Also, we were told that placing Jamie in a school out of the borough would mean he would no longer be under local authority care. We felt very uncomfortable with this.

It seemed we were right that our local school would be the best place for Jamie to start his schooling. It had a good reputation and Sam was obviously already there and enjoyed it. It was a small school with just one class per year – in fact, due to a low birth rate that year, Jamie's class would be smaller still.

I met with the head teacher to discuss Jamie a number of times but on our first meeting I stressed I felt the key to making this work was the school *wanting* Jamie to go there. That his going there was not seen as a problem, or any teachers felt he would be a burden to the class. She agreed, with the right support, she thought it would work.

The right support included a statement of educational needs as it was then known. Getting the statement was a task in itself and one that is, I'm sure, the bane of most parents' who have children with special needs, lives.

Unlike other children with undiagnosed special needs, or those whose special needs are hard to define, Jamie had a recognised *disability*. That in itself should make the process easier. Of course, these things are never quite as straightforward as you hope.

Cliff and I knew it was going to be a slog so we began filling out forms and attending and requesting assessments the year before he actually started school. We realised there was a fine art to it and even attended meetings about how to fill out statement applications. We learned if certain parts of the statement didn't include details of the support he required – quantified and backed-up by professionals – then he would lose out. For example, if we didn't spell out exactly how much speech therapy, help with personal hygiene or fine motor practice he should have each day, in hours and minutes, it may not be included in his statement and therefore he wouldn't receive help with those things.

One sticking point for us was speech therapy. We wanted to make sure speech therapy was included because the statement, as a legal document, would at least give us some kind of back-up should it be needed. For a year the statement went backwards and forwards to the health authority who refused to acknowledge it had to say in writing Jamie should have speech therapy provided by a 'qualified speech therapist' and would not quantify the amount of input he would receive. We fought long and hard and even considered taking it to tribunal. But, after much deliberating we agreed to compromise. In the wording of the statement, we accepted the *regular monitoring* line in return for them agreeing *qualified*. We also spoke to the school and arranged for Geraldine to continue to work with Jamie once a week within school.

STATEMENT OR EDUCATION, HEALTH AND CARE PLAN

The advice and information given here is based on the education system within the UK.

As of 2014 what is referred to as a statement was renamed an Education, Health and Care Plan (EHCP) This is a formal document detailing a child's learning difficulties and the help that will be given.

The majority of children with Down syndrome will require a statement to ensure they get the right help and support at school.

The first stage in the process is called a statutory assessment that is carried out by the local authority. This is a detailed investigation into your child's learning needs. The school or a parent can ask for a statutory assessment. If a school asks for one, they must inform the parents.

After a request for an assessment, the local authority has six weeks to decide whether to go ahead. During this time, it will seek the views of the parents and the school. If an assessment is necessary, the local authority will then seek the views of:

- your child's school
- an educational psychologist
- a doctor
- social services (if your child is known to them)
- the parents

You will be told within twelve weeks whether or not a statement will be made. If it is, you'll be shown a draft and asked for any comments.

If you disagree with the local authority's decision (your child is not offered a statement or the support isn't enough) you can appeal – how to do this will be explained in the local authority's letter. Do not be intimidated by this process, get advice and support from other people who have been through an appeal. Before anything goes to appeal you will be offered mediation that may help. Any appeal should be lodged within two months of the local authority decision.

Once a statement is made, it will be in six parts. These are:

- name and contact details of your child
- details of your child's SEN
- what help your child should get, and learning goals
- what part your child's school will play
- your child's non-educational needs
- how these non-educational needs will be met.

Once your child has a statement, you have a right to say which school they should attend. The local authority will send you details of suitable schools in your area. Some may be special schools, but most will probably be mainstream schools because the education system aims to meet most special needs within this setting.

Time to talk

Having Down syndrome means you are very likely to have difficulties with communication. This can include clarity of speech, being understood, understanding language, and conveying meaning through language. Jamie also had low-level hearing loss as well as processing issues, and low muscle tone – all common in children that have Down syndrome and all factors that can make learning to talk harder. Communication can be so difficult for our children, not to mention frustrating. Therefore, you would assume children like Jamie would be at the top of the list of those needing support and input from a speech therapist. But, as the years have slipped by – and the speech therapists come and gone – I realised this wasn't the case.

Early on we had a wonderful NHS speech therapist who saw Jamie regularly. She had set up the training for local parents to learn Signalong. She tried her hardest to get our children the service they deserved and to offer the intervention the children in our borough needed. She encouraged parents to fight for the service, she set up a support group to try to make better use of her time, and, more importantly she got to know the children she worked with. But it was a losing battle, with constant budget cuts and lack of resources. In the end, it got the better of her and she left. After that Jamie's speech therapy became sporadic and often a waste of time.

When he was a toddler, myself and other parents were involved in lobbying local Members of Parliament (MPs) to address the lack of speech therapy. One of our arguments was if the government would only spend a fraction of the money they spend on pre-birth detection and abortion of children with Down syndrome, on training and maintaining speech therapists instead, children like Jamie would stand a fighting chance of communicating effectively enough to become a valued part of society. I'm not anti-abortion at all, I strongly believe in individual choice. But the lack of funding for positive input and support was frustrating.

The government was very good at juggling figures it seemed. In fact, our local MP told us millions were spent on funding for children with special needs. What the MP couldn't tell us was how much of this went to helping our children – those children with Down syndrome.

Much of the money allocated to Down syndrome is pre-birth – and that meant testing, abortion and counselling for those who terminate the pregnancy.

I remember one rather depressing meeting at a local support group, where the head of speech therapy at the time – trying to placate the group of frustrated parents – told us the local authority would not have enough qualified speech therapists for at least ten years.

Ten years!? Jamie would be leaving school by then.

By the time Jamie was due to start school he was not getting quality or quantity through the NHS. With temporary speech therapists coming and going and nobody working within the team who knew Jamie that well, each time they came it was like starting from the beginning.

One morning when Jamie was around four or five years old he came toddling into the kitchen after breakfast– still with his slightly drunken walk – and said:

"Muu, where ba ball gone?" while signing ball with a puzzled look on his face.

We had a quick hunt and there the ball was under the table. He bent down to where I was pointing and clapped.

"Dank u! Oh boy, dank u!" He was always mimicking the Americanisms from the *Barney* videos he loved to watch and seemed to get the timing and use right every time. This always made me laugh.

He then walked over to me and planted a very wet, slobbery kiss on my face. He had a funny way of kissing when he was younger – always open mouthed and always using his tongue. Almost a lick-kiss. A little surprising to some people, but we'd got used to it. His tongue was still quite big in his mouth then but he was working on keeping it under control.

That same day we had an appointment with a new speech therapist – the first time we'd seen anyone for six months. It was the last appointment we had before he started school so I was keen to know what would happen once he started school.

After working with Jamie for half an hour, she informed me Jamie had a two-to-three-word vocabulary (could only string two to three words together sensibly). He had little understanding of concepts such as *under, on* and *what is?* She also inferred his attention span was short as he was bored after fifteen minutes.

"I'll write a report to let the school know and give them some little exercises to work on," she explained cheerily.

"Yes, thank you. But just to say, he is talking much more than this and I don't think half an hour is really long enough with someone he doesn't know." I was trying to be calm and polite.

"Yes, I'm sure. So, what do you want to do? A block of six half-hour sessions in the clinic with you, or we can show his new support assistant what to do and she can do it daily with him?"

I couldn't hide my frustration. I tried to patiently explain that six half-hour sessions would achieve very little since it would take at least that long for Jamie to trust her and work with her.

"It takes seven years to train as a speech therapist doesn't it? How can a support assistant learn to do it properly in just one session?"

"Oh, we will monitor them, don't worry," she said, clearly oblivious to the irony of what she was saying.

As we got up to leave I felt I had to stick up for Jamie some more. Knowing he picked up on negative feelings from people I didn't want him to feel he hadn't done well.

"Your signing is amazing isn't it, JJ? You are so clever and really doing so well," I said directly to him – signing *'clever boy'* and *'signs'*.

The speech therapist agreed and smiled at Jamie.

I came away disheartened but not surprised. I was just thankful we had Geraldine who was going to continue to work with Jamie weekly at school. I wished people like the speech therapist could see him working with Geraldine for an hour at a time, see him reading his favourite *Preston Pig* books, along with her.

Geraldine would sit on the floor with him with the book on her lap, he would be following the words with his fingers. *Ssh, Don't Tell Mr Wolf* was a particular favourite and he knew it off by heart.

"Where's Preston?" Geraldine would ask, signing and exaggerating her expression and tone.

Pointing to his lips and making a shushing sound, Jamie would excitedly try to turn the page as quick as he could:

"Ohn't tell oolf," he would sign and say the words as best he could.

Each time Geraldine would encourage him and repeat the line with him signing all the while. It was a joy to hear him talking and enjoying books. He'd even bring them in to conversation at other times too and we'd all join in with "and suddenly ..." and pretend to be scared if he jumped out on us. He was really beginning to develop a cheeky personality and he loved to show off. As I listened to their interaction, when they worked together, I would be so grateful for her input.

So, yes, I agreed with the speech therapist that day. He did need to work on areas of his speech, and work he did. Shame the local NHS was not prepared to put in the work to help him.

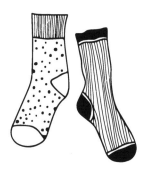

CHAPTER 7

THEN THERE WERE FIVE

Jamie became a big brother when he was four-and-a-half. Meeting Louise for the first time he was a bit overwhelmed, climbing on to his aunty's lap as she held Louise, trying to get her attention back on to him. He wasn't sure what to make of this new baby but was also intrigued, especially as we were all giving her so much attention. He quickly cottoned on this was the way forward and soon enough was smothering her in licky kisses.

When she came home from hospital he would often approach her when she was in her baby rocker or car seat and, twisting his head to the side, look over the top of his glasses and say: *"E-oh baby,"* all the while knowing we were watching him. He would then play up his part, stroking her head and asking, *"Osat?"* as he poked at her.

"Be gentle, Jamie," Cliff would remind him.

"Jentul JJ," he repeated, rubbing her head a little more.

When he first heard her cry he was a little shocked and covered his ears shaking his head but again it didn't take him long to realise he didn't have to worry. He loved to sing to her – especially Barney songs – and mimicked her when she hiccupped. He was still slightly wobbly when he walked so we had to watch out if she was lying on the floor, especially if he was running as we were never quite sure if he'd stop in time.

He soon got used to her though and with his speech coming along it felt he was growing up in to a spirited little boy. His speech was improving all the time and the signing really helped build his confidence and reduce the frustration when we couldn't quite get the word he was trying to say.

I also noticed how much he loved to talk to himself. I'd often hear him having full conversations to himself. He would use such intonation and expression I was in no doubt the 'babble' was real words we just couldn't understand. This was something Jamie continued to do as he got older and I wondered if it was part of how he processed things. He also used self-talk to help himself 'do' things and work out what was happening next.

"Befust, den Barnee," he would mutter in the mornings, knowing he was not allowed to watch *Barney* until after he had eaten.

Knowing what was coming up was also something we soon realised was really important to Jamie. It was almost as if he had to know there was an end to everything, especially things he didn't particularly want to do. He hated being told "wait and see" – not because he couldn't wait to see, but because he couldn't understand the concept of not knowing. He would always want to know that after he had completed something he didn't want to do (brush his teeth) there would be something he did want to do (watch television). This followed through to school with the use of his visual timetable. Everyone soon picked up the sign for *'next'* or *'after'* and realised it was a great way to motivate him.

VISUAL TIMETABLES

As visual learners, who understand what they see better than what they hear, children with Down syndrome really benefit from visual supports such as visual timetables. They help them understand routine, aid memory and gives reassurance, confirmation and can reduce anxiety.

You can make visual timetables very easily yourself either with real photographs – Jamie always preferred real images – or using computer images such as clip art or PECS (picture exchange communication system). Make sure the image looks as realistic as the thing you are trying to represent though, otherwise it will not make sense or be misleading.

Find an image to represent each key activity they do during the day (have breakfast, get dressed, get your coat on, get in the car, go to school etc.) and cut all the pictures to size. Laminate and attach pieces of Velcro to the back of each one. Get a larger piece of card and stick a piece of corresponding Velcro to it. Then simply stick the separate images on to the large card in the order they are going to happen. You can add the days of the week or a clock if your child is able to understand this, or simply a picture of the sun to show day and the moon to show night time. As you finish each activity your child can remove the image if they wish.

Visual timetables are also great for teaching things like getting dressed, brushing teeth and toileting. You can break the tasks down in to smaller steps and the child can follow them.

(www.twinkl.co.uk/resources/class-management/daily-routine/visual-timetable)

Sister, sister

Just as when Sam was little, when Louise was a baby I questioned what it must be like to have a brother that has Down syndrome. Being the youngest child gave her a different outlook. Jamie had started at a local mainstream primary school just a few months after she was born, therefore I had some time to just devote to her. Both of the boys adored their little sister straight away and it would be fair to say she became the family princess – a role she cherished and made her own.

She was the spitting image of Sam, with the same dark, shiny hair, same shaped eyes (although hers are hazel coloured like her dad's) and nose and possibly her dad's chin there somewhere. But in temperament she's very different to both of her brothers. She wears her heart on her sleeve – if you've upset her, you know it and if you've made her happy she's quick to show it too. She was a very happy baby – apart from the colic, we try not to dwell on the colic …

She was subjected to quite a lot of Jamie love early on that, to even the most robust baby, could be a bit of a shock. Huge, slobbery kisses, extra big hugs, lots of attention, and not all of it good. When Louise started sitting up Jamie used to push her over a lot – I'm sure he thought, *"hang on, that's not right, you're supposed to be lying down"* and would just go over to her and give her a shove.

He also seemed to like the fact she screamed whenever he did it. As a five-year-old he was very fond of making loud, impulsive noises, sometimes it seemed, just for the hell of it. Especially if he got a response. Which he always would with Louise. He didn't care if it was a good or bad response, as long as it was a response. So often it felt like a screaming match in the house.

While I would always reprimand Jamie if he was too heavy-handed, I tried not to make a big fuss. Louise soon figured out she could manipulate some situations to her advantage and it would be fair to say she quickly had him wrapped around her finger.

She learned how to get attention and stop Jamie getting on her nerves. First, by screaming the minute he came near her, later on, by saying, "Go away" in a cuter-than-cute voice. There were times when Jamie was unsure of what to make of her. She liked Jamie to chase her around the living room. I would hear Jamie shouting, *"I'mgonnergetcha"* and Lou would be giggling hysterically. Inevitably he would catch up with her, she would fall over and promptly burst into tears. Despite her cries – and almost smothering her – Jamie would carry on. I would then have to intervene, but, two seconds later and she would be back on her feet, give him her cheeky grin and start running again. I wondered why he bothered!

There were times I felt guilty and of course sorry for her if Jamie had hurt her – albeit without intention. He was still quite wobbly on his feet himself as a five-year-old and didn't realise his own strength. I know she had more than her fair share of knocks due to his heavy-handedness. But I tried to judge the situation and not jump in too quickly. Jamie had to learn she was smaller than he was and be gentler and understand she would cry quicker. He doted on her and she knew it.

At first, the concept of her brother having Down syndrome and what this meant hadn't occurred to Lou. As she got older she never questioned why Jamie couldn't do things, just asked how we could help him. She tells me friends ask, "what's wrong with your brother?" Her response is always the same: "There's nothing wrong with him. He's got Down Syndrome that's all."

She has his back.

Talking really early, sleeping through the night, walking before she was three. Cliff and I jokingly called her a miracle child. We sadly lost a baby in the early stages of pregnancy the year before Louise was born, so she was also the child we thought we couldn't have. She was an easy baby in comparison to Jamie, and in fact Sam. Having Louise restored my faith in what being a 'normal' mum was really like.

It wasn't long before Louise could do things Jamie still struggled with. I wondered how she – and he – felt about that.

But they both coped with it. If Jamie couldn't figure out the climbing frame on holiday, Lou would scuttle to the top and talk him up. If he couldn't work out how to switch something on, she'd do it for him.

As Louise got older, just like Sam, she would watch out for him. She would tell him off if he turned the television up too loud or for being too rough. She would also interpret for him and often understood what he was saying when I couldn't. Like Sam, she showed a lot of interest in learning Signalong and would always ask for another new sign to learn.

Sam was seven-and-a-half when Louise was born and by this time was proving to be a great big brother with Jamie in many ways. He acted as an interpreter when others didn't know what Jamie was saying or what he needed. He copied the '*first you do this and then you can watch Barney*' mantra we all did to get Jamie to do anything as a toddler. He would play games he knew Jamie was able to play even though he was probably bored, and he watched far too many tedious videos to keep Jamie happy. That poor boy has seen more *Barney* than any brother should have to.

There were also times when he has been too much like a parent.

There's a trait it seems is common among children with Down syndrome, fondly called being a 'runner' (see *Chapter 8 Running us ragged*). This basically means Jamie is prone to run off randomly sometimes. Be it at home, at the shops, or at the airport ("no Mum, don't worry, we did NOT lose Jamie at an airport, just mislaid him for a while …").

This would often, and understandably, panic Sam.

I lost count of the number of times we would be out shopping and one minute Jamie would be happily toddling along with us – or even sitting in his buggy – the next minute he'd be off and running down the road.

"Mum, quick he's running again!" Sam would yell and start running too.

Of course, Jamie would think this was hilarious and try to go faster.

"Mum! He'll get lost!" Sam would get quite worried and be cross with me for not reacting faster.

I would *usually* be in control of the situation and try to reassure Sam that Jamie was just testing us, and to ignore him. I also only let Jamie out of a vice-like grip when we were well away from danger of roads or areas we were not familiar with. However, there were definitely times I was grateful for his young legs and watchful eyes.

It would have been easy to depend on him, as he was and is such a great big brother. I tried not to, and both Cliff and I made an effort to give him lots of space and time to be Sam as he was growing up. We often told him how proud we were of him. I wondered if he would always have been this patient? Or if having a brother with special needs has shaped him. Of course, we'll never know.

The three of them share a bond that is special to them. Of course, I wonder if they will remain as close as they grow up. But who doesn't wonder that about their children?

I hope the responsibility – and I know there is a responsibility – of Jamie isn't too much for Lou and Sam to bear. When he is older, and we are unable to care for Jamie, I hope, by then, he is able to care for himself to some degree and is not regarded as a burden on them.

This guilt of making them responsible, just by birth, never goes away. *Will they resent us? Will they want to include Jamie in their lives? And if not, what happens to him if they can't?* These are all questions I could torture myself with. But I don't. I choose not to. There is no point. We are all born into a family we didn't choose. We learn to accept them, or we don't.

What both Cliff and I want for all of them is to accept each other for who they are; to support each other's needs and take time to understand what that means. We want them to develop an awareness of the differences between each other, to respect these differences and to help each other along the way. Not to judge each other harshly and be aware of each other's and other people's feelings. Most of all I want them to like each other enough to pick up the phone once in a while. That's just our family values. We would want that regardless of our situation.

Are we normal?

"If there was a magic pill that Jamie could take that would mean he no longer had Down syndrome would you want him to take it?" A question I asked Cliff around this time.

"Yes," was his emphatic response.

"Why?" I asked, surprised at his quick answer.

"Because then he wouldn't have to struggle so much and rely on other people all his life," was his straightforward reply.

I could see Cliff's point completely. If Jamie didn't have Down syndrome he wouldn't have to struggle so much. He wouldn't always be fighting against a prejudice. He wouldn't have to work so hard to learn new things and wouldn't need other people's help so much – ours, doctors', physiotherapists', speech therapists', the local government's and so on.

"Jamie's extra chromosome is an intrinsic part of him though. If it were 'fixed' it would be like taking away a part of him," I reasoned. "You're assuming that Jamie will always be reliant on others to help him?"

This made me feel uncomfortable. I sincerely hoped that one day he would be independent. The fact was, for me, if Jamie was what society classed as 'normal' then he wouldn't be Jamie any more would he?

"Do you think we are a 'normal' family?" was the next question I asked Cliff.

"Yes. We just have to work harder than other normal families."

Again, I disagreed. I didn't feel we were normal — whatever that meant. Maybe I meant typical? Having a child with special needs, I think, places us *outside* the norm, but *inside* another group of people who exist in normal society and try their best to fit in.

As a dad, Cliff has always been very hands-on. He gets involved. He took turns pacing the floor at night when Sam refused to sleep for his first two years, he changed nappies, he was as involved as his job allowed him to be. Sadly, Cliff's parents died in their fifties of cancer. One thing I've always admired is that he hasn't let this define him, or ever appeared to be a 'victim' of what was essentially a real shit hand of cards. But, I'm sure losing his own dad so young has made him understand the importance of his role — maybe more so than most. He doesn't take it for granted. I only knew Cliff's dad for a year before he passed away and never met his mum so I didn't know that side of his life really. He has talked about them and it is clear he was close to both his parents and has a great deal of respect for the morals and values they instilled, including working hard for your family and being a good role model. Cliff can be quite arrogant and has a lot of self-confidence that, from what I've heard are traits inherited from his dad. In fact, Cliff is quite proud of this and will say they have certainly served him well over the years.

Cliff always left me to steer most things regarding Jamie – I kept track of his medical appointments, kept up to date with any developments within Down syndrome and followed up anything I thought worth pursuing. This has put a lot of pressure and a lot of responsibility on me. Sometimes this has been hard to bear as I wished I could just sit back and let someone else look for the answers. However, in reality I knew I was happier being in control than I would have been taking a back seat. Cliff would always step up when I needed him to. Times when I was worrying about Jamie's behaviour or development and my usual internet hunt will have made my concerns worse or just added to the confusion, I knew I could turn to Cliff for some much-needed reassurance. This is what he is good at. He is much less emotional about things and looks for answers. He would often ease the worry or take control of the situation if necessary by suggesting a specialist or professional we could talk to and we would go together to see them.

He has always been particularly good at times when I felt I was being fobbed off and got answers when I have been too close to the problem to be effective. He has played bad cop when we've needed to address difficult issues at school especially when we've had to say, 'no this isn't working, you need to do more.' He doesn't worry if people like him or not and has just demanded the best for Jamie. I do too, but I tend to worry that we'll be seen as too pushy and I have an inherent need to be liked. He doesn't care!

He is a huge support in this way. He has stepped up when necessary and has surprised me with his handling of the situation and the results achieved. Few things really bother Cliff. He doesn't get upset with some of the stuff that I find difficult to cope with – like Jamie not being included when friends were over to play. He was happy to let Jamie watch a millionth TV show if that was what he wants, whereas I would stress that he was watching too much TV. We work as a team. However, unlike in his day-to-day job, he's not the team leader, I am. He doesn't need to talk tactics all the time, he just needs to know what his role is and how I want him to do it. He is supportive, realistic, a sounding board and Jamie's idol.

He has never let Jamie or me down when it comes to supporting us. And he has taught Jamie so much that I never could have. The real, everyday, dad stuff – stuff that his dad taught him – like how to bowl a cricket ball properly. *Apparently, Jamie shows real signs of talent, for that Cliff takes full credit.* Jamie loves being with his dad and misses him terribly when he is away working. Sometimes this can be very galling; especially when I've been up every night for a week.

The fact that Jamie has Down syndrome seems to be immaterial to Cliff and yet he'd prefer it if it wasn't causing Jamie the issues that it does. Jamie is Jamie and he wants what's best for HIM.

CHAPTER 8

RUNNING US RAGGED

When talking to other parents of children with Down syndrome, the subject of whether your child was or is a 'runner' seems to always come up. It appears you either have a runner or you don't – there is no in-between. Jamie was – is? – a runner.

A runner is an affectionate term parents give to those children who like to run away. Not packing their suitcases, leaving-home-type running away. Just the fact that he can run out on you at any given time, anywhere, for no reason, just for the fun of it, running away.

When Jamie was a toddler he would often run off while we were out shopping. He would scoot out of a shop door before you had time to touch the first clothes rack, or pick up a tin of beans from the supermarket shelf. He could untangle himself from my vice-like grip while we were walking along the street. That boy could run fast when he chose to.

Just before Louise was born we moved to a new house, a large bungalow that had a huge back garden. One of the reasons we chose this house was that we could see a larger back garden could offer Jamie some kind of independent living in the future. We also knew all three kids would love having so much space to play in.

However, what we didn't realise was the fun it could offer Jamie. One of Jamie's favourite times to run was when he was meant to be in the back garden playing. But he would not run around IN the garden. Oh no.

With a mischievous streak growing as quickly as he was, one of his favourite tricks would be to pretend to go out to play in the garden then run around the side of the house and out toward the street through the front garden. Not only did the house have a big back garden it had a pretty big front garden, so this was not a short distance. It was like a temptation he just couldn't resist. He'd pelt off when he thought no one was looking (but of course he knew we all were and this was part of the fun). As he took off, either myself or any other adult (and sometimes child) would leg it after him shouting at his back to stop. We quickly tuned into this running habit and learned to weigh up potential runner situations, and acted accordingly. We had a new gate fitted to the side of the house that we could lock shut and big metal gates at the end of the driveway.

After a few months of settling into the house and having had the gates fitted, the running incidents seemed to have lessened. So much so we began to think he'd grown out of that particular stage. But, he was just testing us to see if we were up to the job because, as with many things, he wasn't quite as done with that idea as we thought he was.

One day just after Louise was born, I was at home busy cleaning up the house while Louise was sleeping, Sam was playing and Jamie was watching television. After five minutes or so, my 'mum's sixth sense' prompted me to check on Jamie. *This is a sixth sense I think most mums develop soon after giving birth – it's like you grow a new part of your brain that tells you when something is just not right. Usually it's when things go a little too quiet.*

When I looked, Jamie was nowhere to be seen – and the back door was wide open. I would have usually had all the doors locked, but, as I say, we had relaxed a little. I flew out of the house, shouting at Sam to stay with Louise, unsure which way to go first. Running on to the street I miraculously caught sight of the back of him about 200 metres along the road. He was heading towards the park not far from our house – pushing a pink doll's buggy someone had given us for Louise.

Thank God, he isn't in the road. I thought before sprinting after him.

As I ran down the road, my neighbour, who was in his driveway, gave me a very strange look (I was wearing my slippers) and I puffed a quick "hi there!". I managed to catch up with him just as he entered the park and marched him back home. On my way back past my neighbour, with a completely unfazed Jamie happily padding along in his socks next to me pushing the pink buggy, my neighbour stopped me:

"Is everything okay?" he asked pointing at Jamie, in his socks.

"Err, yes, now it is. Jamie left the house without me knowing and gave me a bit of a scare," I explained, trying to look less flustered.

"Oh, I wondered if he was with anyone when I saw him go past. I like his buggy," my neighbour replied, winking at Jamie.

I laughed along at his joke but politely asked him to stop Jamie if he ever saw him out on his own (on an escape attempt) again.

"In fact, you have my full permission to pin him down on the ground if you need to!" The neighbour smiled nervously and went back indoors.

Of course, I told Jamie off for running away, and tried to explain he shouldn't leave the house on his own. But he didn't care. He didn't see what all the fuss was about.

I was recalling the story to Cliff later that evening.

"What if I hadn't noticed he'd gone as quickly as I had? What if he'd gone in to the road? What if someone else picked him up?" I was building myself up in to a huge guilt trip.

"Nothing happened though, so calm down." Cliff tried to reassure me, but I was still shaky from the whole incident.

"But, we do need to go back to locking the doors, don't we? I wonder why he took the buggy though?" Cliff was half laughing, half puzzled.

"He often does it when there's something to push doesn't he?" I said.

"Yes, I always have a feeling he's going to run off whenever he grabs that push-along car he likes."

Cliff was right, whenever he found something he could push – be it Louise's tiny doll's buggy, her real size buggy or a push-along car – it seemed to trigger something in Jamie's head that made him want to go out into the street.

"We'll just have to turn the house in to Fort Knox."

We both knew he was only half joking.

Up to his tricks

Knowing all about his previous escape attempts, my parents and sisters were always on 'run watch' when they were around too. Perversely, this could be quite funny to witness as they were not as practised at it as us, and so were often a bit over-careful. As he climbed out the car, they would fling themselves in front of him, just in case. If he headed for the house when they were in the garden with him, they would shout a war-like warning that Jamie could be on his way out of the gate and everyone would literally jump into position. We were like an army preparing for battle. Of course, Jamie was completely oblivious and carried on with his own merry thing.

One particular time, my eldest sister Michelle and her partner Mario were visiting and I had an errand to run. They were both great with all three kids so when I asked if I could pop out they of course were happy to help. I returned after no more than half an hour, and I could tell something was up before I'd even got my coat off.

"I've just had a complete nightmare with Jamie," Michelle said looking very pale and a little flustered.

"Just after you left I went to see Jamie in his room and he wasn't there. You'd literally just left." She was breathless trying to tell me the story.

"I remember you shouting out the door was unlocked so of course I went in to panic mode. I checked Sam's room and shouted down to Mario who was in the garden with Sam and Lou."

"All I heard was, 'Mario I can't find Jamie!'" Mario joined in the story, laughing at the ridiculousness of it.

Apparently, within minutes, they had a search party organised. Sam and Michelle ran to the park, but no Jamie.

Mario was told to check the garden (even though he would have seen Jamie go past him?) But there was, according to them all, no sign of him.

"I even sent Sam back to the park to check again," Michelle said.

"I asked a lady who was walking her dog if she'd seen a boy with blonde hair as we'd lost him," Sam said, clearly finding the whole situation quite exciting.

"She asked where I lived and everything. I think she might come around soon to see if we've found him," Sam laughed.

As she was recalling the story I could see Michelle had seriously panicked as she kept darting looks at Jamie, who was now sitting with Louise watching *Barney*.

"I just didn't know what to do, I was so worried. I decided to go around the house one more time and went in to Sam's room – I'd been in there already, more than once! As I was about to leave I just caught a movement out of the corner of my eye. Those bloody cabin beds!"

Sam had a tall, cabin-style bed so it was not always easy to tell if anyone was up there. But sure enough, when she climbed the ladder, there was Jamie grinning away.

"I'd been round the whole house calling his name. Nothing. No answer."

"Oh yes, he doesn't answer when you call him," I told her sheepishly. "It's his new game."

I did feel guilty she'd been put through all this hassle while I popped to the shop. It was hard for other people to look after him. I was used to it. Not everyone else was. This made finding reliable 'babysitters' even more difficult.

I know Jamie's 'running' was small fry compared to other children's exploits. I've heard about little ones that have got out of the house in the middle of the night. Parents only being aware of it when they have been woken by hammering on the door and someone standing there with their child in tow. Another little boy squeezed through a fanlight window in a bathroom while on holiday and his poor mum had the whole of the resort staff looking for him. Then there was the family whose child had escaped, again in the middle of the night, got into his neighbour's house through a cat flap and started the neighbour's dogs barking – this alerted his parents to the fact he was missing. And yes, all of these families have locks, bolts and alarms fitted in various forms.

It seems this extra chromosome our children have gives some of them superhuman abilities when it comes to sussing out how to undo a locked, bolted and sensored door. Burglars in the making maybe?

Luckily, as Jamie grew older, the running incidents did decrease. They didn't actually stop completely until … well, let's not tempt fate eh?

CHALLENGING BEHAVIOUR

As with all children, those with Down syndrome can show some challenging behaviours. The difference between theirs and a 'neuro-typical' child is that they may continue longer and may impact their everyday life more. In fact, 'challenging behaviour' in itself is defined by Down Syndrome International as behaviour that results "... in self-injury or injury of others, causes damage to the physical environment, interferes with the acquisition of new skills, and/or socially isolates the learner ..." (library.down-syndrome.org/en-us/research-practice/11/2/addressing-challenging-behaviour-down-syndrome-applied-behaviour-analysis-assessment-intervention)

If you are experiencing behaviour issues with your child there are a number of things you can do. Firstly, try to establish there is not an underlying medical or health reason for their behaviour. Have their ears, throat, eyes checked. Are they constipated? Could they be anaemic or is their thyroid not functioning correctly? Whilst this may sound dramatic, our children find communicating problems within their bodies hard so it's difficult to know when something physiological is bothering them.

Once you've ruled out any medical or health issues it's time to consider social and emotional issues. Are they anxious, worried or stressed about a situation? This would show if the behaviour was more prevalent, say during lunchtime at school or before going to the shops (which they may find overwhelming) for example. If this is the case you need to work at ways to help them cope and deal with stressful situations.

If you have ruled out all the above – and even if you haven't and there is a reason for their behaviour – it still needs to be dealt with.

Visual aids (stop signs at doorways), verbal cues (say the same thing before you leave "you must hold Mummy's hand at all times or get in the buggy"), signing (sign 'stop' and 'mummy'). It is vital to be consistent and clear about expectations and consequences again using visual aids where you can (a sticker chart worked really well for Jamie).

There is also lots of information online through the various Down syndrome associations offering advice and help.

(www.ndss.org/resources/managing-behavior)

(www.kcdsg.org/files/content/How%20to%20stop%20Runners.pdf)

CHAPTER 9

STARTING SCHOOL

The September before he turned five, Jamie started big school. Dressed in his grey trousers and white polo shirt, complete with red fleece emblazoned with the school's logo he really looked the part. Unable to tie laces, he had a smart pair of Velcro shoes and with his blonde hair now in a neat pageboy cut and his funky gold glasses, he looked quite pleased with himself as I took photos of both the boys on his first day.

"Are you excited, J?" I asked for the hundredth time.

I'd talked to him about what going to school meant and that he would be learning things, playing, listening to teachers and so on. I don't think much of it went in though. As with all things, Jamie was more able to understand through doing, abstract ideas are hard for him to figure out.

He was joining the reception class with just four other children. Another six were due to join after Christmas. It really was a low birth rate year as usually the class would be full of thirty children.

Although his statement was still yet to be signed off thanks to the disagreement about speech, it was agreed he could start school with the full support as was suggested, which was a relief. This meant the school could employ someone as his support assistant (SA) all day. As his class year was so small the nursery nurse who would have been working in the class was given the job as Jamie's SA.

This immediately rang alarm bells with us as we worried she was so used to being a *class* support she would slip back into that role. Also, with the teacher (and school) used to having two staff members in the class I worried they would treat his SA as a class assistant still. But we could only hope for the best.

His first few months went okay. He seemed to enjoy himself and he made slow, but steady progress with his work and he started to recognise letters and numbers and began to attempt to write his name. But there were many small irritations on a weekly basis.

He had a communication book his SA and/or teacher would fill in on a daily basis (in theory) and often at the end of the day I'd read *'Jamie fell asleep during circle time today'* or *'Jamie didn't want to sit on the carpet today'.* If I asked for more details they were often not forthcoming.

"Maybe he's not engaged during circle time or doesn't understand what's going on?" I suggested to his SA one morning when I dropped him off.

"Well he has to learn to sit still with the other children" was pretty much the response I'd get.

I agreed, of course he had to learn to follow rules and routine, but it was frustrating me that no one seemed to realise he may need things changed slightly.

"Do you give him any visual clues about what's going to happen next?"

I'd been asking for months for a visual timetable to be used regularly as it helped Jamie know what was coming next.

I was never quite sure if they were using one or not.

As a visual learner, I often referred to Jamie's mind as like a video. It seemed to me he recorded information all day long in his head, stored it away and when he wanted to, he would 'rewind' and play it back. I knew he was doing this as it was often accompanied by chatter to himself about the particular thing he was 'rewinding' – I called this his rewind time. In that first year at school, I explained the video theory and asked that, after doing new or hard work, Jamie was given 'rewind time' as it was often the key to him remembering something new. Being able to go over what he had just learned without any pressure, no questions, just time to 'watch' and hopefully cement his understanding of it. But I wasn't sure he was being given this time.

Overall, he was doing okay. He seemed to have picked up on the routines of the school day and expectations like where to put his bag, when to line up and so on.

One of the most difficult things I found was there seemed to be a lack of empathy regarding personal issues. Jamie continued to have toileting accidents during his first year so he had spare clothes in school at all times. I would cringe when, at the end of the day the member of staff assigned to seeing him out would walk down the path towards me carrying a plastic bag and announce openly his soiled clothes were inside. Depending on who it was would determine how much detail I would get.

"Could we perhaps discuss this another time?" I said on numerous occasions, painfully aware of the other parents and children within earshot.

I mentioned this to his teacher a number of times, asking that personal issues be discussed in private. She tried her best, but it felt to me Jamie overwhelmed her. She was reassuring in meetings, telling us he was happy in class and doing fine; but she never seemed convincing. It was like talking to someone about France when they'd only ever been to Spain – she knew in principle what we were talking about but didn't ever really want to go there.

The head teacher was also the SENCO – the Special Educational Needs Coordinator. This meant she had overall responsibility for making sure the needs of any child in the school with special needs were being met. She had told me numerous times about the two 'Down syndrome children' she had 'had' before and how she understood how best to help them.

I had doubts when she told me during the second term Jamie was too tired and perhaps he should do half days. Her previous experience obviously hadn't taught her about the shutting down process most of our kids practise when they are finding things a bit tough. If they think they can't do something, rather than try, they'll give up. Often using distraction techniques, like sleeping, or bad behaviour (or even extra nice behaviour) to get out of doing it.

I was in her office a lot. I lost count of the number of meetings I had about everything from the way the older children keep patting him on the head, to why he'd not progressed with his reading.

Each time I was struck by one thing. Lack of knowledge – hers and her staff.

Despite asking repeatedly that staff attend specific courses, or contact agencies we knew could give them the right help, the school still seemed unwilling to learn. They would listen politely, nod their heads in the right places and then carry on as before, with maybe a minor adjustment to keep us off their backs for a while.

It really felt they were just 'coping' with Jamie at school.

Making friends

Throughout that first year at school, Jamie made friends with Jonathan. A quiet boy, Jonathan had taken it upon himself to help Jamie in a number of ways without being asked, and they seemed to have hit it off straight away and had a genuine friendship. *'Jonathan showed Jamie where to take the register today'* was the kind of thing I'd read in his communication book.

After a month or so of getting to know each other at school, as is perfectly normal with children of that age, Jonathan asked if he could come to our house and play after school one day. While I was really happy with the idea of Jamie spending time with friends, I had my reservations. It wasn't I didn't want him to have playdates. It was just …

It was tricky. Whenever we had children round to the house he didn't really play *with* them as such. As this was usually friends' children who were visiting me it wasn't so much of an issue. But a friend coming specifically to play *with* Jamie, that was different.

Every day, when Jamie came home from school he needed his 'chilling time' and every day the routine was the same. He would walk through the door and head for the television. He would pick out a video from his box, take his shoes off and settle down for his 'fix'. More often than not, this fix would be *Barney*, but it could be a few other videos too. He had a huge collection of videos and knew every single one of them off by heart. He preferred singing and dancing videos and loved to dance along with each one. Often, before the first video had ended, he would line up the next, anxious he wouldn't be allowed to watch another one. If he had his own way, he would watch his videos all night long.

When he was watching his after-school videos there were a number of factors that could determine whether he got to watch another video straight away or not: if Sam wanted to watch something he would have to share the television; if Lou needed something and so my attention was elsewhere; how the dinner was going, how tired he was, and so on.

If I didn't allow him to watch another video, I would have to prepare myself. Be ready for the onslaught of whining and moaning that was relentless, noisy and soul destroying. Crying, moaning, constantly turning the television on behind my back, emptying the video cases and so on.

Of course, my worry was if he had a friend round he would not have this downtime he so desperately needed. But I agreed to give it a go, especially as Jamie seemed keen too. Having spoken to Jonathan's mum she was very relaxed about it and we agreed a day the following week.

As the day approached I prepared for it in a way I never had with any of Sam's playdates. I checked with Sam to make sure he was going to be at home, and asked if he'd step in if Jamie wouldn't play. I thought about the games Jamie would like to play with Jonathan and made sure they were out ready for them. On the day itself I made sure Lou would be ready for a nap for some of the time so I could be around to manage things if they got tricky.

Jamie came out of school grinning clutching Jonathan's hand and was signing *'my house'* before he even reached me. Jonathan was also excited and we headed home with both of them giggling in the back seat of the car.

"Come on J, let's show Jonathan your bedroom," I encouraged as soon as they'd taken off their coats and shoes.

"Is Barney, is kip. Is Weese oom." He showed off his beloved Barney, his bed and then his sister's room, pointing out all his favourite things as he led Jonathan around the house finally stopping in front of the television and his boxes of videos. He started to empty them out telling Jonathan in jumbled excited babble about each one. After a few minutes of letting him do this I suggested they play a game.

"Yeah, come on J, let's play cars," Jonathan said and Jamie jumped up and they headed to his room together.

I was so pleased he wasn't moaning or refusing and they lasted a whole ten minutes in the room playing together. The rest of the playdate I had to chivvy Jamie along a bit and suggest games they could both play as some of the games Jonathan suggested would have been difficult for Jamie. Sam popped in and out to help keep them amused and when Louise woke up from her nap we all ended up building a den from sheets, blankets and chairs. While I was in the kitchen preparing dinner the two boys, dressed up as pirates, both came in tapping their elbows.

"Ditdit," Jamie said. He wanted a biscuit.

I couldn't resist them both as they stood signing and saying biscuits to me. I gave them their biscuits and off they went to sit in their den, I could hear their giggles and smiled to myself.

When his mum came to collect him, Jonathan seemed to go home happy, Jamie seemed happy so I was happy. It had been a success.

Playmates and playdates

At the beginning of the next term, the mum of another boy in Jamie's class, George, asked if Jamie would like to go to their house to play one day. Now this was a completely new ball game, and one where I was not sure I knew the rules. Laura was a very understanding lady who I often chatted to and she always asked how Jamie was doing at school. She seemed caring, sensitive and a good laugh and was one of the parents who clearly thought Jamie added something to the class (they didn't all feel that I'm sorry to say). George was a lovely boy too. A bit more boisterous than Jonathan but he had a heart of gold and a hint of mischievousness I loved. I'd seen he and Jamie got along well and enjoyed each other's company.

Laura suggested she take Jamie to their house to play. We chatted about it and I tried to be positive but knew there were things I had to make clear.

"Jamie is still learning to take himself to the toilet," I said a little embarrassed.

"No problem, George is the same, I always have to remind him."

"Oh, yes, but you might need to actually take him. He might need help, or, won't know where to go, or flush the loo ..." I was jumbling my words out by this point and knew I sounded like an overanxious mother.

I explained he liked his downtime when he got home.

"No problem," she said. "He and George can watch television together."

Despite the reassurances I was nervous.

Seeing my doubts, she then suggested maybe they could take Jamie to the park right by their house.

By now I knew I was sounding far too weird so I said I'd speak to Jamie and get back to her. I swear she thought I was bat crazy.

That night I told Cliff about the invitation and he was clearly not as bothered by it as I was.

"But what if they get in and he starts ransacking the place for *Barney* videos, you know he does that at people's houses right?" I tried to explain.

"What if she takes him to the toilet and he won't go. Or she might leave it too long and he will go, but in the wrong place. Oh God, imagine if he does that?"

Cliff sat and half listened. I think he switched off at some point.

"I don't know if the park would be better or his house. He likes the park, doesn't he? But only if he can play cricket. He might wander off; do I tell her that? Ah this is too hard."

"Why don't you just let him give it a go. You could be worrying for nothing." Cliff, as ever, was being pragmatic. But at that moment this was as helpful to me as a chocolate teapot.

Was I this anxious when Sam had his first playdate I wondered?

I wasn't, but it's hard to see clearly when you're overthinking everything. Things felt so much more complicated with Jamie.

I was very conscious of treating all three children the same, of setting the same rules for all of them. They followed the same game plan.

But this situation made me question myself. Did they really?

"Ah, Mum, Jamie's watching *Barney* again and I want to watch my programme. It's not fair, he always has the television on what he wants," Sam would often say.

"Sam, you've got a television in your own room, not to mention a PSP and a PlayStation® AND a DVD player. Jamie doesn't and I can't distract him right now so you'll have to find something else to do."

But was this the right way to deal with it? Was I fobbing Sam off?

I tried to be neutral and sometimes I could cope with the amazing whining Jamie could do just so Sam or Lou could watch what they wanted to on the big television in the living room. Other times I couldn't – whether this was because I was busy doing something or because it had simply been a long night with little sleep.

Yes, Sam did a lot Jamie didn't do – either because Jamie wasn't interested, or he was too young. Sam had friends over a lot. He went out with his dad and with me on his own to do 'big boys stuff'. He did all the things a young boy does. But I wonder if all he wanted was to come home, switch on the television, kick off his shoes and watch a video? As Lou was getting older, the same would happen.

So, with that in mind, perhaps encouraging Jamie to see friends after school wasn't such a bad thing. Perhaps I could ask George to come here and ask Laura too, then she can see Jamie at home – and more importantly, I can see her, seeing Jamie!

Overprotective? Me?

"Do I sound like an overprotective mother?" I asked Cliff, he didn't answer. Tired from a long day at work and lack of sleep, which was showing in the flecks of grey hair and dark circles under his eyes, he was by now sick of me talking about it.

I didn't want to be that kind of person. I seemed to be though. It was so frustrating. I had to stop overthinking.

So, I asked Jamie.

"J, do you want to go to George's house one day to play? You know, after school, like Jonathan did here?" I signed too, to help him understand what I was saying.

I asked a number of times. Sometimes he answered yes, sometimes he said *Barney*. Sometimes he just ignored me.

And that was the other thing which worried me. How would Laura know what he was saying?

If I – or anyone – asked how his day at school went, Jamie would either nod and put his head down or simply say *Barney*. Often if someone asked him a question he would answer *Barney*. When he was worried about something, he said *Barney*.

To Jamie, 'Barney' meant *'hang on a minute, I didn't quite get that. Oh, you are looking at me so you must want an answer. Oh God, I don't know what you mean, or what I should say, or how to say it. I know ... Barney.'*

It was like a comfort blanket. It was familiar, he felt safe when it was near.

Decision made

After talking to Jamie and agreeing it was a good idea for George to come to us, I told Laura of my plans when we saw each other at school the next morning.

"You know, Jo; the idea was maybe to give you a break. It would be nice for him and George to play by themselves for a while too don't you think? But of course, that's fine. You take George home Friday and I'll come up for a cuppa; that would be lovely."

She was smiling the whole time and looking at me with unnervingly understanding, kind eyes. She was without a doubt being genuine. I came away feeling a bit silly and, of course, like an overprotective mother.

Friday came along and I reminded Jamie before school George was coming home with us that day. I also put a note in his communication book so his SA could remind him. I let Sam know so he didn't ask one of his friends round too. I prepared dinner early, and I prepped Louise just as I had when Jonathan came.

They both came out of school holding hands and trotted down the path to meet me. Once home, George spotted the climbing frame, and excitedly asked if they could play in the garden. Jamie on the other hand asked for *Barney*, but I herded him down the garden telling him to go play. While I was dumping bags, coats, folders, and getting Louise sorted, I heard the back door open and Jamie came clumping through.

He stomped over to the video completely oblivious to the fact he'd just left his friend outside and cheerfully sorted out which one he wanted to watch.

"No," I told him, "George has come to play with you."

George came wandering in and after a little persuasion – and a bit of bribery in the form of a biscuit – he and George went into his bedroom to play.

For the next half an hour I went back and forth from his room, directing him like an actor.

"Get your Play-Doh™ out Jamie, what about the cars? George, do you want to play hide and seek? Come on Jamie you count and we'll hide."

By the time Laura came, I was exhausted from the effort of getting Jamie to play. He did okay though, and I managed to keep the telly off for nearly an hour. I made Laura a cup of tea – a peace offering – and let Jamie put a video on. George and Lou got on with emptying cars out of a box.

I explained to Laura again that Jamie liked his television time – a lot. I told her he was tired after school and so needed a bit of downtime.

"It's the first thing George does too when he gets in, switches on the television. I'm sure they'll be fine if Jamie came to our house, you know George would love that."

We chatted about signing, and how she had always wanted to learn it.

When she left, I felt I'd made up for my overanxiousness and she understood the reasons for my worries. I was sure Jamie would go to theirs to play very soon and when he did, yes, I would still worry. But he would still go.

A few weeks later, Jamie went to George's house to play and did indeed ask to watch *Barney* whilst he was there and rifled through their whole DVD collection without finding what he wanted. But he coped and from what he and Laura told me when I went along to collect him, he had a lovely time. They'd watched a bit of television together, played in the garden and generally had fun and George said he'd like him to go back one day.

CHAPTER 10

SPORTS DAY

Although not a sporty child myself – I never took the winning medal in anything apart from the wheelbarrow race – I remember sports day being great fun when I was at school. The fact we got to spend the afternoon running around the school field, the shouting and chanting that went on and also having my parents there to cheer us on, always made for a fun day.

It was in Jamie's first year at school that sports day had been re-introduced. Before then, the head had decided it would be better to have a sports afternoon, where it was less competitive. More of an exercise in exercise.

Therefore, when it was brought back as more of a traditional sports day, I was looking forward to going along to enjoy the day with the boys. There were to be field events in the morning that meant jumping and throwing, and track in the afternoon

– a sprinting race and a longer run for the older kids and a just-for-fun relay for all.

I've never been all that competitive when it comes to sports – possibly because I was so bad at them – as a result I guess I'm fairly relaxed about it. I encourage my children to take part and congratulate them on trying their best (even when I suspect they haven't). I want them to enjoy winning, but I also want them to accept losing with grace, and perhaps learn something from losing.

"Don't forget, PMA," I tell both boys the morning of sports day.

"Yep, positive, mental, attitude, I know, Mum," Sam replied half laughing half rolling his eyes.

PMA was a family saying we'd drummed into Sam from a young age and is pretty much all my 'pep talk' would usually consist of. That and '*have fun*'.

Sam was always naturally athletic. He played football, basketball and cricket at school and, when his dad dragged him out on the golf course with him, turned his hand to that pretty well too. He had been chosen to compete in the long jump at sports day and was very excited. I'd planned to join the activities at lunchtime just for the afternoon events. But Sam's excitement was catching, so Lou and I went along earlier and stood on the school field most of the day. Sam came second in his event and I was enthusiastic in my congratulations. Although I knew he would have loved to win, he seemed happy with second place. He buzzed around the field all morning, thoroughly enjoying himself.

Jamie and his classmates were taking part in an individual running race and a relay later in the afternoon. I had spoken to him that morning about how he would be '*running*' at school, and I would be coming along to watch.

"*Welca to a sembly,*" he said nodding happily.

This was because the last time I had been in to school was to watch his class assembly the week before where he'd been practising for weeks to welcome everyone to their assembly and he was a little confused by what was happening that day.

When he came out for lunch, and was pointed in our direction he was excited to see us waiting for him and joined Lou, Sam and I for lunch. After he'd eaten his usual: sandwich and grapes with an apple juice, he ran off to play with his friends, joining in the 'practice' races with some of the older kids up and down the newly painted track.

"Ha! Ha! Look at Jamie running!" I heard one of the older kids shout.

"Don't laugh at Jamie," his friend said, aware of me sitting close by.

"I'm not, he's …" and he trailed off. The poor boy looked a bit embarrassed as he looked over to us and pretended not to have heard.

I knew he wasn't being unkind. He didn't mean *Ha! Ha!* I genuinely didn't think he was laughing AT Jamie. I think what he meant was *look at him trying*. To me, it seemed that was how most people saw it when Jamie joined in anything competitive at mainstream school, "ah bless him for trying".

Yes, this could be annoying but people weren't being unkind or trying to be hurtful. They just couldn't see past the fact Jamie had Down syndrome and therefore didn't see him as Jamie first. It's a problem Jamie will always have to deal with, getting people to see beyond his 'disability'.

When the time came for Jamie's race, he lined up with his friends and I jumped up ready to cheer him on.

He ran straight down the track, didn't veer to the side and didn't trip or fall. He was smiling the whole way and when he got to the end, he received a huge clap – in fact, it was the biggest clap of the day so far. He came last. I – and everyone around me – cheered like he came first. You see, with Jamie it really is all about the taking part and he started with PMA. I hoped one day he would come further up the field. But, at that point in time, I was just delighted he made it without falling and without going the wrong way. Little steps and big lessons.

Later that afternoon, a parent next to me shouted out to her son; "Sean, where did you come?"

Her son pretended not to hear her. He had come last and his mum knew it. Eventually when it was obvious his mum wasn't giving up, he turned around and shrugged his shoulders.

"Last? Last? That's rubbish, we don't do last!" she shouted to his back. "What's the point in running at all if you're going to come last?" She looked at me and laughed, oblivious to the irony.

I wondered to myself what it must be like to be that person. If all you cared about was winning? Would they have felt the same pride I had with Jamie?

The relay race was the final event of the afternoon and each class took their turn. Sam's team won and he was delighted and proudly showed off his winning rosette. Being the youngest class, Jamie's was the last to run and when the time came he got up ready with his team. Running his little legs off, still not as steady as his classmates and made even more difficult by a fairly bumpy running track, he did well to stay in his lane. He had been told to give the baton to his classmate which he did no problem. But, as the second runner took off, Jamie took off with him.

With much laughter from all of us in the crowd his poor SA started to chase after him;

"Stop Jamie, stop running, stooooopppp!" she shouted to his back.

But, he was having too much fun and with the cheers from the other children getting louder, egging him on, he made it to the end before another member of staff grabbed him to stop him sprinting back again. It really was quite funny watching him sprinting after the girl in front with his SA sprinting after him trying to stop him.

I laughed along with everyone else. After all, clearly no one had 'told' him he should stop running halfway along the track this time. It was like watching a *Tom and Jerry* chase and everyone there could see the hilarity of it.

At the end of the afternoon, Jamie was tired but happy. He came home with a 'well done' sticker like the rest of his class. Sam was pleased with himself for winning his relay race and coming second in the long jump. I told him how proud I was of him and signed lots of *'clever boy'* and *'fun day'* to Jamie.

I came away feeling lucky; I had the best of both worlds. My children knew how to take part and enjoy it. They could win or lose AND enjoy it.

I wondered how those other parents felt.

Sticks and stones

After a number of people had commented on how much Louise looked like Sam as a baby we decided to watch some old family videos so they could see for themselves. Louise was just over a year old, Sam was around eight and Jamie almost six. Cliff was away travelling with work, and the children all missed him so I thought it might be a good way to fill the gap for them.

Sam loved watching the images of his first birthday. Being spoilt rotten with lots of presents, and all my family clamouring for his attention. We saw some footage of him with a broken arm at seventeen months old; quite a sorry sight as he was very wobbly from the weight of the cast. We chatted about how he had done it – he had been screaming in his cot, refusing to go to sleep. When he realised I wasn't going to succumb to his screams he tried to climb out of his cot and fell out. Not my finest parenting moment but we laughed at the story and he enjoyed hearing what he had been like as a baby.

With their dark hair, round faces and large brown eyes we agreed Sam and Louise were very alike as babies and joked at how Sam had inherited his dad's strong jawline – a standing family joke.

We then put on a tape of Jamie at about seven months old. Jamie hadn't ever been dark; his hair was very blonde and his skin tone olive like mine. He looked different to the other two as a baby. We watched baby Jamie on screen, his head still wobbly, and the careful way he was always propped up against something so he didn't topple over. The video showed us celebrating his christening where he was wearing a cream raw-silk romper suit, the same one Sam had worn for his christening, and despite all the fuss around him was happily oblivious to the occasion. As the image of me holding him flashed up on screen, a familiar finger of pain wound its way through my stomach. Feelings of such fierce protectiveness. I looked over and tears were falling down Sam's face.

I knew what was wrong before he said anything because I felt it too. I went over to him and put my arms round him. He snuffled a bit, wiped snot over his sleeve and tried to talk. He was obviously feeling uncomfortable. Eventually it spilled out of him.

"It's the Down syndrome," he said guiltily, like he was telling tales, speaking the words I knew were so hard for him to say.

"I love Jamie and I love he's my brother, but I just sometimes wish he didn't have Down syndrome all the time."

I was so proud of Sam for being able to express this. I really didn't mind it may be hurtful for me to hear. I did mind it may be hurting him.

He told me some kids in his class had been laughing at Jamie and the way he talked.

"They say your brother just babbles like a baby and I hate it," he said tearfully. "People keep asking me 'what's wrong with your brother?' And I don't like it."

"What do you say?" I asked him.

"That there's nothing wrong with him, he's got Down syndrome," Sam said, puckering his mouth and raising his eyebrows like it was obvious.

With a lump in my throat and a rock in my stomach, I comforted him.

"I sometimes wish it would go away too Sam," I told him. "I wish you, as his brother, didn't have to feel sad about it or worry about it. But it's not all bad is it? Just think, we have lots of good things come out of having Jamie too. After all, we get to queue jump at Disneyland!"

We both laughed as we remembered the special treatment we'd got when we visited Disneyland Paris the year before.

We talked about the fact Jamie wouldn't be *our Jamie* if he didn't have Down syndrome. I also said, as gently as I could that, although it's hard, it is not going to go away and Jamie would always have this 'label' as it were. The mood lightened and with Jamie and Lou clambering around us wondering what was going on, Sam smiled and said how he loved having a brother and a sister and in fact, he'd quite like another (I flinch).

I wondered if he meant he wanted another 'normal' brother – something I understood. Cliff and I had considered it. We had always joked about having at least three children, but once Jamie was born it was more daunting, and at the same time more necessary. We talked about how we wanted Sam to have a sibling he could look to for support with Jamie if he needed it. Someone who understood what it was like having a sibling with special needs and yes, as they got older, someone who could help take the weight of this from his shoulders. However in reality, just like Louise, even if we were to have another child it wouldn't have helped Sam at that moment. That child would have been a baby when Sam needed a playmate and someone to take the flak.

Later that evening after Louise and Jamie had gone to bed, Sam and I had a cuddle together on the sofa and we talked about why these kids might be saying such horrible things.

"They probably don't really understand what they are saying, or how it makes you feel," I tried to explain.

But of course, he worried; we all worry about what our peers think of us don't we?

Sam was always a very sensitive, empathic boy and young man. It was this sensitive nature that made it so hard for him to listen to people saying those things. Just before he went to bed he was desperate to reassure me he loved Jamie to bits and he didn't care what others say really.

"I always stick up for him, Mum, I always would. I don't care what they say."

We finished the conversation hatching plans on what he might say next time he felt awkward, and yes, what he might say that would make *them* feel bad about their words too. I agree with him when he says: "They're just stupid."

Maybe not the most grown-up thing to do but hey, I am only human.

SIBLINGS

Being a brother or a sister of a child with special needs can be tough. It can also be tough as a parent knowing this. There are some ways to ensure they feel as special if you are concerned they feel left out or isolated, or if you are worried about them.

- Set aside some time to do something with just them. I know this can be hard, especially if you can't get help with your child that has Down syndrome. Ask grandparents, friends and so on to help if you can.
- Speak to all of your children about Down syndrome and what it actually means. They may have fears that are unfounded or ideas about what having Down syndrome means that are worrying them.
- Assure them that it is okay to be upset, annoyed, embarrassed, angry or resentful at their brother or sister as this is perfectly normal in all sibling relationships, Down syndrome or not. They shouldn't feel that just because their sibling has Down syndrome they cannot have the same feelings as they would if they didn't. But ask them to talk to you about those feelings and if necessary get them some outside help to deal with them.
- If you are part of a support group, try to arrange for the siblings to get together. They will have a lot in common and may find an ally to share their fears/stories/pride with.

Obviously if you are really concerned it is worth talking to a professional, maybe a school counsellor or a therapist. Again, approach your local Down Syndrome Association for more information.

(www.nads.org/resources/sibling-resources)

(childmind.org/article/advice-siblings-of-special-needs-kids)

CHAPTER 11

AND SO TO SLEEP

I'm pretty sure high on any parents list of gripes or frustrations is sleep – or lack of it. Most parents have stories of bed hopping with their spouses and the kids, sick children up all night and the various techniques used to get some sleep. However, I'm one hundred per cent sure every parent or carer of child with Down syndrome have enough stories to fill a library. It is the question guaranteed to be asked at any meeting, gathering or random exchange in a street.

"Does your son/daughter sleep?"

So, this is it – the sleeping chapter. How it was for us and how we coped. Be warned, it will be of no help whatsoever. My apologies for this in advance but I know it's important to share.

When Jamie was a baby, he slept well. In fact, so well, we would have to wake him up to feed and dress him. He slept loudly (snuffling like a pig), but for long periods of time. When he was very young his snuffling was so bad and his chest got so congested he needed to be upright at night; so he slept in his car seat for a short while, as I said earlier. As he got past six months old, his sleeping pattern changed, as all children's do. He began waking more in the night and needing comfort, he didn't settle very easily and always needed someone with him until he fell asleep. At about eighteen months old, he went in for a minor operation to bring down an undescended testis. After that things changed dramatically.

Although we can't be sure the operation had anything to do with it, it is the only event we can remember before Jamie stopped sleeping. On reflection, I can see we were building up to sleep issues for a long time, if not in the middle of them, but ignoring them. There were many big changes that year, he started playschool, Sam had started school and we were coping with having lost a baby through miscarriage. But at this particular point in time, he simply stopped sleeping. Getting him to bed became a huge struggle. In fact, that is an understatement. It became a mountain to climb every single night.

We would have to wait until he was sound asleep in our laps before, very carefully, taking him up to bed. This was a bad habit that continued longer than it should have and of course didn't help with his bedtime routine. But throughout his early years we found we were still doing this as we had exhausted all other ways of getting him to bed.

We had tried all the usual ideas of leaving a door open, light on, music playing, sitting with him but not touching, sitting holding his hand, ignoring him, jumping up if he made any noise. None of it worked. The stealth-like creep to his room was comical to watch – if you didn't have to do it. Without waking him, either me or Cliff would scoop him up from the sofa where he would have nodded off, more often than not holding his bottle, and carry him sound asleep to his room. No one was allowed to speak, move or blink an eye, just in case it woke him mid-creep. We knew which stairs creaked and so stepped gingerly round them, we knew the door could make a slightly too loud shussing sound on the carpet if pushed too quickly, we knew to hold him until the very last moment when we would have his blanket and sheets fully surrounding him before sliding our, by now, aching arms, out and making our retreat. This also had to be stealth-like.

Once safely back downstairs, there would be an audible sigh of relief. Maybe even a glass of wine before inevitably the sound of Jamie crying would start. Sometimes he would wake just a few times in the night, say every two hours. Sometimes he would be awake within ten minutes of going to sleep – then continue this pattern all night long.

When Jamie was around two we moved into a larger house and his bedroom was just across the hallway from us. We also bought him a new bed. It was a child's bed and was fitted with one of those temporary safety rails to stop him rolling out. At eighteen months old Sam had fallen out of his cot and broken his wrist one night. We were wary of something similar happening to Jamie so had decided to move him in to a 'big boys bed' shortly after the move. In the middle of the night we became used to hearing his heavy footsteps thudding across the landing. Half asleep, we would steal ourselves for the slam of the door that always came just as he entered our room. He couldn't gently push a door open, or in fact, just come in the door as it was – it was always half open. On the nights where we had managed to drift off into a naive slumber, the slam of the door would literally make us jump awake. I'm amazed our hearts didn't give out on us at times. There Jamie would be, standing in the doorway, rubbing his face and looking at us as if to say, "Where were you? I'm up. Now what?"

The general routine would then be that one of us would go back with him to his room and try to get him back to sleep. More often than not, when Cliff did it, he would fall asleep on the bed with him and I'd find them both there in the morning. Cliff's long legs bent almost in half and his arms hanging out the side of Jamie's single bed. When it was my turn, I'd stay awake, unable to sleep in the bed with him (and also aware this wouldn't help) and try to creep out, but he would wake up again within minutes of my leaving the room. In the end, for the sake of a few hours' sleep we would let him sleep with us.

We tried everything over the years to try to get him to sleep on his own. One method, controlled crying, involved leaving him to cry if and when he woke up and leaving longer periods of time between going in and reassuring him – without picking him up. The 'experts' were very strict about this. When you are as sleep deprived as we were you will try anything. We tried ignoring him completely, reassured by said experts he will eventually drop off, exhausted. The crying would do him no harm and he'd eventually settle. Err, no. What actually happened was he would just get more and more upset and scream louder and louder, until we could bear it no more.

Was two hours long enough? Did we give in too soon?

It obviously disturbed Sam's sleep too and probably our neighbours'. But we felt we had to try. This was a huge fail.

We tried drugs – the legal kind. After discussions with his paediatrician, Jamie was prescribed sedatives. These were to help him relax and so get to sleep in the first place. The medicine was meant to work for four to six hours. We gave him the medicine before he went to bed, only to be woken four hours later. We tried giving it to him just before we went to bed, thinking at least we would get a few hours solid sleep. That didn't work either, he would still wake after just a few hours.

He was tested for sleep apnoea, something that is quite common in children with Down syndrome. This involved him being wired up to a machine all night long – basically to see if he stopped breathing during his sleep. Keeping him still that night so the wires stayed attached was not easy. In fact, Cliff spent the night on the floor next to his bed, re-attaching any wires that came loose. We hoped the results would give the reason why he couldn't stay asleep. But, no, the results showed he didn't have sleep apnoea. He just seemed very restless throughout the night, fidgeting constantly. His preferred sleeping position was to be bent over double, with his legs under his chin. To look at him you would assume this was too uncomfortable. But apparently not.

We finally accepted the fact he was just a bad sleeper and we just didn't know why. We had got used to the routine of him falling asleep in the living room, and then taking him to bed, very carefully. He generally would sleep for an hour or so at least and if he woke during the evening, one of us would put him back to bed (very annoying in the middle of a film). Then, once we were in bed, when he woke, Cliff and I would take it in turns to sleep in his bed with him. That way we each got a half-decent night's sleep every other night and didn't disturb anyone else. It wasn't ideal and caused a lot of strain and a number of arguments, but it was the best we could do at the time.

Crocodile tears

Just as we thought we'd found a way to cope with the sleep issues, one night, about halfway through his first year at school, Jamie jolted awake, pretty much as soon as we put him in his bed. Once awake, he cried until we brought him back in the living room with us. I was worried – and bloody annoyed.

We wondered if he was unwell.

"Are you poorly Jamie? Does your tummy hurt?" I asked him signing *'hurt'* over his tummy area.

I had tried to help him understand what 'having a poorly' was or, what it meant if something hurt as he never seemed to tell us if he felt unwell or had hurt himself. Some weeks before, he had fallen over and grazed his knee. On that occasion, I

SLEEP APNOEA

Apnoea, which literally means 'without breath' is the term used when someone stops breathing for very short periods of time, usually ten to twenty seconds. In children, sleep apnoea is almost always obstructive. During an apnoeic episode, the child will have decreased oxygenation of the blood. Symptoms of Obstructive Sleep Apnoea (OSA) are: snoring, restless/disturbed sleep, frequent partial or total wakenings and daytime mouth breathing. Some children with OSA have odd sleep positions, often with their neck bent backwards, or even in a sitting position. Some children with OSA sweat profusely during sleep. Some children will have daytime grumpiness or sleepiness, but it's not common. Some children may have noisy swallowing as well.

It's actually quite common and millions of people are affected by it. The causes can vary, but for children with Down syndrome, these may include enlarged tonsils and adenoids and poor tone in the tongue. In general, the main cause is the tongue falling into the back of the throat.

The best way to diagnose sleep apnoea is through a sleep study.

Sleep apnoea is treatable and can be quite simple. The treatments are determined depending on sleep study results. Home Continuous Positive Airway Pressure (CPAP) is usually the treatment of choice and is tolerated by children very well. This is administered by a nasal mask or tube during sleep. The tube/mask administers air with an amount of pressure designed to keep the airway open. There is usually a period of getting used to the treatment but afterwards the child will notice the positive difference and come to want their CPAP.

(www.ndss.org/resources/obstructive-sleep-apnea-syndrome)

made a big fuss of telling him he'd 'hurt' his knee and it 'must feel poorly' and showing him the sign. But I realised he hadn't got the point when, a few days later, shortly after he had been sick, I asked where he was poorly and he promptly rolled up his pyjama trousers and pointed to his knee.

So, it was guesswork most of the time and it was often not until he had been sick, had an upset tummy or we noticed a wound we were aware something was wrong.

I wondered if it was growing pains keeping him awake at night. I recalled Sam having these at around the same age. But despite asking him over and over again what hurt, Jamie still didn't say anything. So, we gave him some medicine and waited for him to drop off.

Again, the next night he woke up really upset soon after being put to bed. When Cliff went into him he became even more upset and it took a while to calm him down. With Cliff losing patience (when Jamie gets really upset, he has a very distressing and quite piercing whine) I took him on my lap and held him tight trying to calm him down. I started to talk to him about nothing in particular; distraction often helped and I felt him relax. It was then he started muttering. Jamie muttered to himself a lot and I could pick up snippets of information from this, seemingly meaningless, chatter. The odd clue as to what he may have enjoyed during the day, what was worrying him and so on.

"Ko dial. No!" he muttered, squirming on my lap.

He carried on making whimpering sounds saying the same thing and I realised he was saying crocodile.

"Do you mean crocodile, Jamie? Like the one in your school book?"

We had read a book he'd brought home that night featuring a crocodile. He started whining again and repeating the word *'ko dial'*. The penny dropped.

"Is the crocodile scary, Jamie?" I asked.

He nodded and hung his head.

"What, the crocodile in your school book, Jamie?"

I tried to keep my voice light; "Is the crocodile horrible? Shall we tell him to go away?"

He looked at me, nodded and said: *"I shoh you."*

He got off my lap, held my hand tightly and we went into his bedroom, bypassing his school bag. I tried to pull him back and get the book bag but he wouldn't let me.

Once in his room he pointed to his bookcase and sure enough, there on the shelf was a book with a crocodile on the front cover. It was a finger puppet type book where the reader's fingers made up the crocodile's long snout. In fact, it was the same book Louise had screamed at the previous week; and was why I had put it away on the shelf in Jamie's room.

With some relief, I made a big show of telling off the crocodile and throwing it out of the door. I told Jamie the crocodile was very silly and would not be allowed back in.

After a while, sitting on my lap, he drifted off to sleep and was put back to bed.

I was annoyed at myself for not having thought of nightmares sooner. Especially as Sam would often have terrifying dreams that woke him when he was seven or eight. As a child myself, I remember I had nightmares that would play on my mind for a long time afterwards – just the result of an overactive imagination.

The thing I hadn't considered was the fact Jamie's imagination could work in the same way. He could make up scary stories in his head and sleep would bring them to life. I guess I had just assumed when he slept, his mind slept too. Why, when he hardly ever rested properly I don't know. His body was constantly on the move when he was 'sleeping' so it goes without saying his brain was active too.

I was not considering his imagination worked in the same way. How arrogant of me to think he wasn't capable of making up stories or scenarios in his head. And he could be as scared of a simple crocodile book, as his little sister was.

I knew that wouldn't be the end of his sleeping problems, and it really wasn't. However, I rested a little easier knowing I now understood a little more about Jamie's world.

The sleep issues continued with us having to carry him to bed after he'd fallen asleep. He still woke in the night, and some weeks and months were worse than others. We'd even have periods where we thought it had improved as he only woke two or three times a night. We never found the ideal solution. We spoke to many experts and tried all the ways we could to get a good night's sleep. Eventually, we resigned ourselves to the fact he just couldn't settle very easily and when he was stressed he needed comfort. Jamie's paediatrician suggested we had to take our cues from him and let him learn to relax in his own way. It was not easy and it meant we rarely had a whole night's sleep. But after exhausting every option we learned to accept this was the way it was.

CHAPTER 12

ONE SMALL STEP

Jamie had started his second year at school, and Sam his fifth. Years 1 and 4 as they are officially known in the UK system. With the niggles we'd had regarding Jamie the previous year, I was determined this year would be different. He had a new teacher and a new SA and I had already decided I would be a lot less concerned with being liked by the school staff, and more concerned with making sure the staff did the job they were supposed to – even if it meant being one of *those* parents. The previous year I think in the back of my mind I had been too worried that if I was too pushy, the school would say he couldn't stay there.

It was with a heavy heart I left Jamie at the school office on his first day in the (very capable) hands of the school secretary. His support assistant hadn't yet arrived and I was disappointed she wasn't there to take Jamie into his class to meet his new teacher. I was trying to be optimistic for this SA as when we'd met at the end of term it seemed she was going to be a good fit. While his classmates walked round the long way (around the school through the playground) – fully aware they were going into a new classroom – Jamie was confused and a bit baffled as to why I kept signing *'new teacher'* and *'wait'* to him every five minutes. But off he went with the secretary quite happily waving to me.

The next morning Jonathan was on hand to walk round with him. There were a couple of boys in his class who tended to look out for him. Not in a patronising way and not because they had been told to (you can spot those kids a mile off). They did it as they knew Jamie sometimes needed a helping hand. When Jonathan waved hello, and offered to walk round with him I was more than happy to let him go the long way around.

That evening Sam had complained he never had time to play with his friends in the playground before going in to registration. His year group had to be in school ten minutes earlier than Jamie and we tended to arrive just in time for him to go in to class. So, on the third day of school we arrived a little earlier. Amazingly we actually made it out of the house on time and having arrived at the gates and said goodbye to Sam, I waited with Jamie.

After a few minutes of watching, Jamie signed *'kiss'* and *'bag'* to me. I looked at the crowd of children flocking round the gate waiting for it to open and said/signed he should wait. He looked at me, looked at the (by now) huge crowd, and gave me a kiss. He took his bags from me and sauntered – slightly unsteadily, as his bag was almost as big as he was thanks to the amount of extra word cards, number cards, books he had – down the path.

The bell went, the crowd rushed forward, I cringed. He stood his ground, refused to be hurried along by the older girls who always clucked round him, and looked back at me. He gave me a nod and grinned.

I watched his blonde head bob through the gate, willing my feet to stay where they were in case they followed him of their own accord. I walked out of the school gate avoiding eye contact with the other mums, and rushed to the fence next to his classroom to check he made it. I waited, and waited, and panicked. Five minutes later, he wobbled around the corner clutching the hand of another little boy in his class. They were both laughing, and dawdling, and being six-year-old boys. Climbing the few steps to the classroom takes a bit longer for Jamie but his friend held back with him, no rushing and no pushing. They saw me watching and both waved happily, then stood at the door and gave it a tug. Tried again, looked at each other, and pondered. They can be heavy doors those classroom doors. The teacher came to their rescue and in they went.

I came home proud, relieved, dumbstruck and very emotional.

One small step for Jamie, one giant step for his mum!

Speaking out of turn

Jamie formed a good relationship with his SA straight away. His teacher appeared enthusiastic and his communication book would tell us some days he did better work than others and seemed a little tired, even falling asleep during some lessons. But overall, he seemed happy. I wrote in his communication book he shouldn't be allowed to switch off during the day, maybe he needed to be engaged a little more. I also spoke to his SA and said he needed pushing, gently but firmly. I still felt the school were just coping and we needed them to do more than cope. We needed them to push him. To give him the confidence in himself to learn to write, read and do all the other things we knew he could do.

Toward the end of the first term in Year 2, the head teacher asked to speak to Geraldine after her weekly session with Jamie. The head teacher apparently asked Geraldine if she thought we had *unrealistic expectations* of Jamie. Geraldine, surprised by the question, told her no she didn't think we did at all, Jamie was quite capable of learning to read and write, with the right support. That our expectations he be supported to do so were more than appropriate.

When Geraldine rang me later that day to tell me about the conversation I was furious. As was Geraldine. The quiet alarm bells that had been playing in the background last year, now rang louder. Especially as I wasn't sure if his teacher had been party to any of this.

I went in to speak to his teacher the next day as I had already built up a good relationship with her and felt she would be more honest with me. She assured me she had not been told about the head teacher's questions and she would speak to her about it and get back to me. She asked if it was possible Geraldine misunderstood her intentions? The teacher was trying to be diplomatic. I said I'd wait to hear back from her.

I strongly felt the conversation with Geraldine came from the standpoint of someone who could see having a child like Jamie in their school meant a lot more than extra funding and an SA. He needed an holistic approach with the whole school doing their bit. Particularly as it was such a small school with just one class per year, everyone had their part to play.

I thought back to a meeting we'd had only recently. I had been in to see the head and asked if the dinner staff could be spoken to as Jamie hadn't been eating properly at lunchtimes.

He had been choosing food I knew he didn't like and so was not eating it. I knew this as his SA had mentioned it in his book. I guessed he was being pressured to choose without really knowing what the choices were. I suggested he be given just two choices and the person serving the food use a visual prompt – after all, the menu was decided in advance and was on a rota so this could be easily planned. Of course, this meant extra effort as someone would have to make up the visual prompts and the lunchtime staff would have to comply. It hadn't happened as far as I was aware.

Therein was the issue. While the head teacher had said to me she welcomed Jamie at the school, the reality of it was perhaps proving to be different. Jamie's statement was often not worth the paper it was written on because many parts were not followed or taken into consideration.

I worried the strain of being the square peg was too much for Jamie sometimes. Although research proves most children with Down syndrome do better socially at mainstream school – they learn appropriate behaviour – they become more adept at fitting into this mainstream world. Some of them even flourish and, shock horror, pass exams like 'normal' kids. But, it seems, this only happens with the right support. And these two magic words are the key to it all.

Following my chat with his teacher, the head teacher asked me in to school and explained she really didn't mean she thought we had too high expectations at all. That she simply wanted to verify with Geraldine that the school's expectations met ours. She said as a professional who had been working with Jamie before he started school she thought she may have some insight in to how to achieve this more effectively.

I politely accepted her explanation and used the opportunity to again request a staff member attend a relevant course. We spoke about using signing more at school and she agreed more staff would benefit from knowing how best to motivate and support Jamie throughout his day.

We agreed we would continue to work together to ensure Jamie's needs were being met appropriately and I stressed to her the importance of speaking to us if she felt there were any issues. For the rest of the school year this was pretty much the case. Jamie made some progress. He began forming some more letters and his counting and reading improved slightly. Still no staff attended any courses.

Always learning

Despite the reluctance of the school to attend conferences I tried to keep abreast of developments in educating children with Down syndrome and so often attended workshops and conferences for parents. One such conference was organised by our local Down Syndrome Association support group. It incorporated workshops and speeches from the Down Syndrome Education Trust (now known as Down Syndrome Education International or DSEI). Sue Buckley, the Trust's then director, was someone I'd heard speak before. I was always struck by her passion and down-to-earth way of looking at things. She has a warm smile and looks like someone's mum (she is too). To listen to her speak was always fascinating and inspiring.

A story Sue shares openly and is one that always shocks was about how, in the early 1970s, she adopted her daughter who has Down syndrome. Her daughter had been living in a hospital for the 'severely subnormal' and the UK law at the time stated she was 'unfit to benefit from education'.

Just forty years ago and children with Down syndrome were thought of as uneducable!

Just take time to digest that for a while.

~

In 1971, the law changed and children could no longer be classed as 'uneducable' – that was when special schools were introduced. What these schools were like, I obviously don't know. I can only guess – and my guess is they were more like day-care centres. Sending children with Down syndrome to *real* school with *normal* children was not an option then.

Sue Buckley was one of the many parents who fought long and hard to change this ridiculous idea. Through years of research, she and the Trust has turned around the way our children are educated. They have discovered so many ways to support and encourage our children, you cannot help but be in awe of them.

At this particular conference, Sue Buckley talked about how, as her daughter reached her thirties, they had been faced with a completely new range of problems and obstacles. Employment, relationships and housing to name but a few. It was clear she firmly believed in treating her daughter the same as her other children, but admitted she often had to remind herself to do so. She talked of sexual relationships – and those of us with younger children cringed at the mere thought of this. She told us about Sarah Duffen, who had learned to drive at twenty-one, and we all felt a sense of pride. In fact, Sarah's father had contacted Sue to tell her of his daughter's reading skills in 1979 and the Trust's head office was named after her.

Going along to these conferences also offered me the chance to meet other parents, many of whom had been through similar experiences and so could relate to my worries, concerns and hopes. We all laughed along as some recounted awkward behaviour in public and sympathised with those having schooling issues. There was a sense of unity because the parents were forward thinking and, like me, wanted their children to achieve their full potential as we knew they could.

Ideas flew around on how best to help our children read. Stories were retold about children who fell to the floor in the middle of the shopping centre and ways we had avoided arrest when resorting to tough parent mode to deal with these meltdowns. In between all of this, we learned new strategies, absorbed ideas and realised how very clever our children can and will be.

There was usually such a positive attitude you couldn't help coming away full of plans of what you could do, and how you could help your child reach their potential. After that particular day ended I felt inspired and determined to get to grips with Jamie's handwriting. I was interested to find out more about hand gyms, conversation diaries and storyboards. I wanted to look at the research papers we had heard about, I needed to buy the book about friendships and social groups.

That night in bed, I couldn't sleep. My mind was buzzing. What should I start first? When could I fit in time for hand gym in between the clubs Jamie attends? Where do I start with the behaviour management, and how do I persuade school to follow my lead?

After tossing and turning for what felt like hours (and a few huffs and puffs from Cliff as I was keeping him awake too) I forced myself to remember the Daffodil Principle (see *Chapter 4 Making progress*).

One bulb at a time, little by little.

I tried to shut my buzzing brain down and finally slept.

The next day, having decided to start with one of the many good ideas I'd learned about, I put together the special box that would become Jamie's 'hand gym'.

In it were balloons, blown up part way and filled with Play-Doh™, pegs clipped to some card, small buttons, squishy balls and other items I knew would be fun to touch, squeeze and fiddle with. The idea behind all these things being it would encourage Jamie to develop the fine motor skills he needed to write. Squeezing the pegs, poking the Play-Doh™ filled balloon and so on. I decorated an old shoe box to keep them all in and then showed Jamie everything with much excitement – being careful to avoid him feeling any pressure to do anything but play.

I even managed to get Jamie to do some homework using his new special box as motivation. I was on a high from the satisfaction of seeing him trying new things but again had to remind myself to think Daffodils.

The rest of what I learned would wait – but just not too long.

Attending conferences like this would open my eyes to the fact Jamie – and we – are very fortunate. It was fantastic to meet such a dedicated team of people who were not willing to give up on our kids. DSEI, and other charities like them, worked long and hard to discover ways to improve the quality of our children's lives. It's hard not to feel humbled. Without them, I wouldn't have been worrying about hand gyms and conversation diaries. Instead, I'm pretty sure I would have only needed to worry about the number of changes of clothes I should pack for Jamie at his day-care centre.

Thank goodness for forward-thinking Sue Buckley and the like! Now I needed to take some of this positivity in to school and encourage the people who worked with Jamie to feel it too.

THE HISTORY OF HOW DOWN SYNDROME WAS 'DISCOVERED'

Years before Down syndrome was officially 'diagnosed' there is evidence of people with Down syndrome in art, science and literature. But it was an English physician called John Langdon Down that first accurately described a person with Down syndrome. In his work published in 1866 he described the condition as a distinct and separate entity to other patients he was working with. The language in that time was shockingly offensive (he worked at the Royal Earlswood Asylum for Idiots) and so further reading is best done through the following websites with the clear knowledge that, thank goodness, we are more sensitive now.

The term 'Mongol' was often used in the early years as Dr Down referred to his patients as having similar facial characteristics to people from the Blumenbach's Mongolian race. This term for the condition became less common after the 1970s due to its inaccuracy and the fact that it was considered pejorative.

It wasn't until the mid-twentieth century that karyotype techniques were discovered, which could be used to help identify the shape and number of chromosomes. In 1959, the French physician Jérôme Lejeune identified Down syndrome as a chromosomal condition. Instead of the usual 46 chromosomes present in each cell, Lejeune observed 47 in the cells of individuals with Down syndrome.

In 2000 an international team of scientists successfully identified and catalogued each of the approximately 329 genes on chromosome 21. This accomplishment opened the door to great advances in Down syndrome research.

(langdondownmuseum.org.uk/dr-john-langdon-down)

(lejeunefoundation.org/)

CHAPTER 13

THAT'S WHAT FRIENDS ARE FOR

The summer holidays can be a trying time for most parents. Keeping the children entertained – and yourself sane – can be a challenge to say the least. When, like my three, the children are different ages and stages, it can be even harder. What will interest the older one is boring for the younger ones and vice versa.

Most school holidays I would meet up with Nic and Sam and their children. Between us we had four girls and three boys, so it was a good mix. I was the only one who had gone for number three so Louise was treated like everyone's little sister.

We'd arranged to meet in a large park nearby and although as a rule Jamie wasn't keen on parks, that year he'd discovered a love for cricket, so as long as there was a chance of playing cricket, he would be okay – for a while.

As soon as we all arrived and got ourselves settled by the large play area, the five older children immediately went off to play. Jamie hung back a little but, with some encouragement and patience from the others, he followed on. Louise stayed with us as she was too young to go off on her own. It wasn't long before he headed back to where we were. Maybe this was because he couldn't run as fast or climb as quick; I didn't mind, they were all there to have fun, and why should everyone else always have to hold back for Jamie?

Nic and Samantha, however, were always aware of this and every now and then, they would gently remind one of the older ones to ask if Jamie wanted to play with them and more often than not one of them would ask on their regular visits back to us and the food and drink supply. Jamie though, seemed happy wandering around the playground on his own and if he was struggling I would go and help him on and off equipment, showing him how to climb something and pushing him on the swings.

At one point as I was pushing Jamie on the swing the three girls came over and asked if I'd like them to push Jamie for me for a while. I smiled at those sweet girls who I'd known from tiny babies and felt so much love for them. Their thoughtfulness touched me. I could tell they felt a bit awkward about it but they wanted to help. I thanked them and said we were fine and they flew off to find another game to play.

During a break for lunch, having seen the boys playing just before, Jamie asked to play ball. As we were all eating I told him to wait. Five minutes later, lunch over, they all sped off again to play but Jamie stayed put. I spotted the boys playing football behind the swings.

"Do you want to play ball now Jamie?" I asked.

"Yeah." He nodded and Nic and I wandered over.

"Let Jamie have a turn." Nic encouraged her son as Jamie ran between he and Sam.

"No, he can't kick it properly; I'm kicking it with Sam."

"That's not true. Come on you know Jamie can kick the ball fine. Practise with them both."

Ted passed the ball without any more discussion and Jamie chased it back to Sam.

"He's so desperate to get better, you know what he's like," Nic said to me as we watched.

Ted had recently joined a football team and was a bit discouraged as he felt he couldn't play as well as the others. We had been talking about it earlier and I understood his reaction. He wanted to play with Sam – who was older and could help him with his skills. I'd even overheard him talking to Sam about how to improve at lunch. It was refreshing we could say to him, 'no, include Jamie' and it happened. That young man went on to be one of Jamie's 'buddies' who always made extra time for him when we met up and took care to really listen when he talked. Those early awkward moments paid off and was testament to the fact that often lack of understanding makes children behave in a certain way and adults have their part to play in helping with acceptance and inclusion.

We ended the day with a game of rounders – a game near enough to cricket to make Jamie happy. He loved it when we all cheered him on as he hit the ball and ran around the pitch.

When I got home, I reflected on the day. Although it was hard work trying to keep Louise and Jamie happy while the older kids played independently we all had a great time. It had been good to see Jamie playing on his own too. He had held his own when he wanted to. He had chosen what he wanted to do. He had managed to climb things I didn't think he could and didn't whine to go home nearly as much as he had done before.

This had a great deal to do with the thoughtfulness of my friends and the way their children accepted and learned to understand Jamie's different needs. When Louise would not leave my side, they would step in and check on Jamie, even though they could have sat down all day and left me to get on with it. They had come over to me when I had been pushing Jamie and Louise on the swings and told me to go and sit down for a while. They interacted with Jamie on a level most people never did. They talked to him and encouraged him. Simple as that. I felt very grateful to have such understanding friends.

Left out

During that same summer, a similar day out had been planned with other friends who I had known since I was at college. Again, we had children of similar ages although just boys. We arranged to meet for a walk and picnic in the local woods and once there, Sam and the other three children immediately started kicking the ball around. Louise sat with us on the picnic rug and Jamie headed for his cricket bat. After struggling for a while to get it out of the bag, he ran over to where the others were playing football.

"Kkit, 'am?" he ran to Sam eagerly, a bit wobbly from the size of the bat.

"Nah, I don't want to play cricket, we're playing football, J, maybe later, yeah?" Sam replied giving him a high five as he ran past.

Jamie sat on his haunches – holding his bat and watched the others. After a while, leaving Louise with my friends, I went over and asked if he'd like me to play cricket with him.

"No!" he said adamantly, dropped the bat, and ran to join in the game of football.

He chased the ball – and the boys – around, but he was always a bit slower than they were. I tried to catch Sam's eye to remind him to include his brother and sent secret mum/son telepathic signals (that sometimes worked!). Not on this occasion though and they were oblivious to Jamie's attempts to join in. No one kicked the ball to him and Jamie continued to run around after them and seemed happy to do so. I decided not to make a big deal out of it and left them to it and went back to join my friends who were sitting down.

Within ten minutes, the boys were bored with football and headed for the sand pit. As they all ran off Jamie was left with a look of bewilderment on his face. I could see him thinking *'where'd they all go?'*

"They've gone to play in the sand Jamie, do you want to go too?" I said as I walked over to him again.

"No, doh wan," he replied shaking his head and sighed.

"Shall we see if Lou wants to play cricket with us, J?" I asked as Louise came toddling over.

"Yeah, cum Weese!" he agreed grabbing his bat and handing me the ball.

The others were running around us as I played with Jamie and Louise, flitting from football, to the sand pit, to climbing, all generally having a great time.

Picnic time and I had to go back to the car to get ours as I hadn't been able to manage it all when we arrived. Louise was tired and hungry by now and insisted on coming with me, but Sam and Jamie were happy to wait with the others. When I came back the rest were all tucking into their food. Jamie was sitting on the picnic blanket, on his own, waiting patiently for his food. The other children, including Sam, were sitting on the bench munching away happily.

I was struck by the way he had been left out of the loop again. Perhaps I was being oversensitive? I chastised myself. Maybe they weren't sure what to give him? So I bit my tongue, laid out our picnic and kept smiling.

After lunch, we packed up our stuff and headed into the woods. The boys were keen to get climbing trees and jumping in mud. Jamie, a little tired by now, didn't want to walk; the effort of walking on unsolid ground was hard work sometimes for him. People often didn't realise the effort it took Jamie to do what other kids his age could do without thinking. Getting them both around the woods was not easy with Lou in the buggy, so I bribed him with the promise of an ice cream at the end of the walk. The others went ahead and after a few false starts, we caught up with everyone just as the rest of the boys stopped to climb a tree.

Jamie was whining a lot by now.

It wasn't long before they were off again and, dragging his feet, I reminded Jamie of the ice cream he was going to get at the end. He relented and ran to catch up with the boys. As he reached them he quickly slapped one of them on the back and shouted, "IT".

The boy shrugged him off and ran away. Jamie ran after him, obviously thinking he was joining in his game of It with him. The boy stopped and again Jamie smacked him on the back.

"Get off, Jamie!" my friend's son said rather crossly.

I realised he thought Jamie was hitting him.

"I think he thought you were playing It with him!" I shouted over. But he just ignored me and ran to catch up with Sam who was far ahead.

"Do you know what, Jamie, I don't think he wants to play It."

Jamie shook his head and said, *"No play"* and slumped to the ground in despair.

I wondered to myself why one of the mums – my supposed friends – didn't step in and encourage one of their boys to play It, at least for a little while. I was also beginning to get cross that Sam wasn't considering his brother's feelings either.

As the others walked off, and Jamie began to whine, I decided to give in. Jamie by now was hunched on the ground, refusing to move. This wasn't worth the fight.

I told my friends to go on with the walk, I would wait for them at the shop. I asked Sam what he wanted to do and he guiltily asked if he could go on with the others. No problem, I said and genuinely it wasn't. I totally understood he'd rather climb trees and run around having fun.

It took me twenty minutes to walk with Jamie and Louise the few minutes back to the shop. Jamie refused to walk, instead he sat on his haunches with his arms firmly crossed saying, *"No walk."* We had a couple of stand offs – where he squatted on the floor wanting to be carried. I refused and carried on walking to just out of his sight and waited. He got a few stares as people walked past wondering whose child this was, sat on his own, apparently lost in the woods, looking so sad. But soon enough they would realise I was mum and would give me either a pitying shake of the head, an embarrassed smile or just ignore me. I tried to ignore the glances as he laid in a pile of mud making a strange, loud, whining noise. In the end, we compromised (well, I gave in) and Jamie got in the buggy while I carried Louise on my hip.

I knew Jamie was tired and fed up and although pushing a buggy through the woods, while carrying another child isn't something I'd recommend to anyone, it was the only way we would get to the shop.

By this time, I was feeling angry, sad, depressed, and frustrated.

I was angry with my friends for not encouraging their children to include Jamie, or seeing how much of a struggle it was for me in this situation. I was angry with Jamie – for what, I couldn't decide. Not joining in? Not wanting to walk?

Not being Sam? I didn't know. I was angry with myself for letting it get to me.

When we finally got to the shop, I bought the ice creams somewhat resentfully and tried to calm down. As we were sitting down to eat them the others arrived back. My friend, surprised we'd only just got ice creams, asked if we'd waited for them. I explained we had only just got there as Jamie had refused to walk.

She asked if I was okay.

"As okay as I can be," I told her.

We left shortly after.

Back at home that afternoon and Nic called for a chat. All of my upset came spilling out. I sobbed down the phone. My worries this was how it would be for Jamie. Always on the outside, always the one children were either told to play with or being left behind. I admitted I worried friends didn't really want to go out with us, as I was too sensitive to how their children were around Jamie. I told her how it had been so hurtful to watch the way Jamie had been ignored that day. I questioned why Sam had not looked out for him a little more.

My dear friend listened. She told me to stop being so hard on myself. She also reminded me not to be so hard on Sam; he was usually more than happy to look out for Jamie. I knew this and knew I wasn't being fair on him. That made me feel even worse.

What happened that day brought up a whole host of fears. Fear this was what it was like for Jamie, always being left behind. Fear he felt inadequate as he couldn't keep up with his peers. Fear I would always feel the need to fight his corner and make sure he is included. Fear of what would happen if I wasn't there to do that.

When I finished on the phone, Jamie – as intuitive as ever – came over to me for a hug. I clung to him with tears rolling down my face. He buried his head in my shoulder and said quietly, *"Barney yes pway."*

That hurt the most. He felt it too. People didn't appreciate how obvious it was to him he was not being included. Being left out did matter to him. Perhaps they thought he didn't have feelings? He did – as did I.

That day, I wondered if I expected too much of other people. I decided for the time being, I would just avoid seeing those particular friends. I didn't need it and couldn't cope with the fall out. What we all needed was to be around friends who at least tried to understand our family – all of us.

CHAPTER 14

BACK TO SCHOOL

With the summer over it was back to school for the boys. Jamie had really got to grips with toilet training over the summer and although he still wore night pants, during the day he was dry and clean. He had made big progress in his speech too, now using sentences much more and signing confidently. His speech was still unclear to those that didn't know him and I knew he'd have to rely on a fair bit of patience as he went in to a new year with a new teacher and SA. I had met Jamie's new teacher at the end of the last term and we had talked about how best to help him progress. She was enthusiastic and I was cautiously optimistic. She told me she was excited about teaching Jamie and was looking forward to learning from him too. So I was feeling positive as he went in to Year 2.

She and his new SA were keen to start a Signalong course, and after we spoke it was clear she had spent time reading as much as she could about teaching children with Down syndrome, and she wasn't afraid to ask questions if she was unsure about something. His SA also seemed great, she tuned into him quickly and initiated a completely new set of resources that suited Jamie perfectly. To top it all, his teacher had said she was keen to attend an education conference for those working with children with Down syndrome and the head teacher had agreed. It was all working out really well. It felt they wanted Jamie to do well, they wanted to see him progress.

One day, after a couple of months, the teacher put a note in his communication book. She proudly wrote that having asked Jamie to read with her that morning, he had stood next to her and gently leant against her. He would do this for support as well as comfort. They had connected and she knew it; she was delighted.

Jamie who was seven that November seemed quite happy at school and had friends he talked about regularly. He was always being hugged by the older girls outside the school gates (*stop babying him*, I would scream silently, while outwardly smiling knowing they didn't mean any harm). The older boys were always wanting to high five him (okay at first, but soon seemed like he was a performing monkey). But Jamie appeared to enjoy all of this. I even began to feel confident. With this kind of support, Jamie could really make some progress this year.

Which he did. But, with this progression, Jamie began to show signs of panic. We had seen this before. When he had an upturn in his learning, it worried him – he could feel the excitement from his teachers and us and would think, '*Whoa there, I'm not that good, let's back off a bit.*' It's as if he didn't believe in himself.

This would show itself in various ways. He would stop doing things he had previously done independently, or shut down during the school day – literally fall asleep. He also began to be less than happy to go to school and his sleep, that was already terrible, became worse. Particularly on a Sunday night.

After a particularly bad Sunday evening, I knew I had to go in to speak to his teacher. When I did, she told me she had noticed a change in his behaviour and wondered if he was feeling pressured. She told me she had already started to pull back a bit, to give him some time to adjust to his progress. I was reassured she had already picked up on the fact he was struggling and she had realised why this may be.

We all tried our best to reassure him. His teacher and SA supported him. But things didn't improve as the term went on. Jamie started coming home from school unhappy. He seemed sad, frustrated, worried and other emotions I couldn't quite put my finger on. Every day at breakfast and dinner, he would ask, *"Kool?"* in a way that suggested he was hoping the answer would be "No, no school today."

He loved Fridays. Not only did he get to have chips at school on a Friday, but he also knew it was the last day before the weekend. Then, come Saturday morning, he would stomp into our room very early – also having done the same at least twice in the middle of the night – and check again: *"Kool?"* There would always be a cheer when the answer was, "No, it's Saturday. The weekend."

School holidays heralded more cheers. He would ask regularly when he would be back at school – always with hope in his voice the answer would be, "Not today." And cheering when it was.

I went into school a number of times over that second term to ask if he was having any problems, if there were any signs of him being unhappy while at school. I asked if they knew what was causing the anxiety. Each time his teacher, head teacher or SA would reassure me they were keeping an eye on him.

I felt lost. Something was bothering him and yet no one could tell me what it was, least of all Jamie.

After one of my many visits, the school told me he was playing by himself a lot, through choice apparently. Their idea was to have a member of staff watch him at playtimes. This was one of the first alarm bells as he was meant to have supervision during playtime and lunchtime already. I raised this with the head teacher and she told me they had decided (without consulting us) he didn't need support at playtimes now. 'To help him become more independent' apparently. Of course, the school failed to see the irony in this. I expressed my concerns that he needed the support and made a mental note to check again.

During the third term, I got a call from school one day to say Jamie wasn't very well and could I go in. I was half expecting a call as there had been a major whining session that morning when he realised it was a school day. He had had over a week off school the week before with a chest infection.

When I went to collect him, he was snuggled into his teacher's lap in the area used as a sick bay, looking very sorry for himself. She explained he had told them he had a poorly tummy. I asked him what was wrong. He signed, 'home'. He then said, "Watch Shek?" (watch Shrek?) I smiled sweetly, took his hand, and took him home. All the way home he asked for one video after the other. I had made my mind up. No videos that day. No matter how much he whined, no matter how difficult the day became. He was going to have to understand coming home ill from school meant rest and boredom.

Although he did lie on his bed for a while once we were home (tired out from the amount of whining?), after an hour or so he was playing with Lou, kicking a balloon around, and asking for bread (so much for the poorly tummy).

Only at half past four, did I give in and let he and his sister watch the television, and only what was on at the time. He didn't like this at all and kept asking for his favourite video. Each time, I said the same thing as I had all day: "No, if Jamie has to come home from school poorly then he has to rest and not watch videos."

By the end of the day, Louise was repeating "poorly, no video" like a mantra.

That evening, by luck, was parents' evening. The ideal opportunity to talk to his teacher about my concerns. She told us (as she had before) he was always happy and settled in class. He was not upset, didn't cause any problems and seemed happy. My next question was playtime – the battleground for any child. Was he playing with other children at playtime? Was he on his own a lot? Did the other children interact with him? His teacher said all was fine.

So, what next? Why was Jamie so worried about going to school and what could we do to help?

Honestly? I was stuck. Yes, he had been slightly under the weather. Yes, he was tired. It was the end of term after all, all the kids were tired. Yes, he would rather be at home where he could watch television and sing along to his music as much as he wanted. But, he couldn't. He had to learn

My gut feeling was it was hard work and he was feeling the pressure. I thought Jamie was going through a 'growing up' stage and his understanding and ability to do things was increasing. Through hard work – and this scared him. He just couldn't believe in himself and his abilities.

School had to push him. Something we fully supported – God knows, he needed pushing. But, he couldn't always cope with the pushing. If only he could see how much he could achieve if he let himself. His teacher and I spoke about ways to push without shoving. I hoped she wouldn't give up on him.

I left the meeting glad she and his SA had seen the panic and knew it wasn't because he couldn't do what they were asking. He just needed time to accept he could. So, they and we were going to have to take it a little more slowly. Let him really cement what he was comfortable with and give him time to process and cope with what he was learning.

That was the last meeting before Jamie moved on to the next year – Year 3. Key stage 2. Was he ready? We hoped so.

Happy places

When Jamie was anxious or worried, one strategy I picked up on that he would use was to go to his 'happy place'. Most of us have a happy place. A place we go to in times of need, a place we feel content. This can be a childhood memory – a holiday perhaps, or a time you felt special, happy and content. It can be a physical place. Somewhere you feel totally at home, where you feel all is right with the world. It can also be an imaginary place; a place in your mind that gives you a feeling of peace.

If Jamie could tell us about his happy place I'm sure his number one place when he was this age would have been Barney, the ever-present purple dinosaur. It was like a comfort blanket to him. There would often be a comment in his school communication book that: "Jamie has said Barney a lot today."

This was often a warning sign he was feeling scared or anxious about a situation and was something that came up a lot in the last term of Year 2.

Barney to Jamie, meant comfort. Watching *Barney* made him feel secure and happy. I'm sure in some ways he got as bored with it as we did, but it was his comfort blanket. Some kids had a beaten-up teddy bear with a missing ear that was old and smelly; Jamie had his *Barney* videos and they meant the world to him. Once the right video was playing, he was in his own world. A world where no one was asking him to do anything he couldn't, or didn't want to do. He knew this world well and was comfortable there. He could join in with every word of every song and every dance. He was full of confidence.

"*Aaaddee, ook,*" he would say to me, still using the word that sounded like daddy but I knew meant me, with such eagerness it was as if it were brand new to him.

"*Ook!*" Insistent that I – or whoever was around – would stop and watch, he would wait, keeping one eye on us to make sure we were actually watching, with a look of such anticipation on his face. Then, when Barney did just what he knew he would do, he would laugh and clap and often burst into song.

He was so happy at times like that, so full of his own cleverness it was a joy to see. But, of course, when I was in the middle of cooking dinner, or helping Louise or Sam with something my patience wouldn't see this and I would simply get frustrated at the fact here we were again watching the same video.

Even as he got older, when he was bored, or simply wanted to switch off, Jamie would stop whatever he was doing and start reciting a song out loud. Wherever he was, whoever was around. He would have to see it through. I found this incredibly frustrating, especially when we were trying to get out of the house or I had other things to do. I hate to think how annoying it was when he was supposed to be reading his book or finishing his spellings at school.

Another favourite thing to do was to watch Sam's dancing shows. Up until Sam was around eleven, he was a keen dancer and Jamie loved to watch him dance. Especially when he was in a show. We would always buy the DVD and Jamie would watch it over and over again. Even though he may have only seen a routine just the once, he would go into school and show his teachers it. Jamie at this age had also begun to dance himself and was part of a dance group where he was learning tap dance, ballet and did some modern dance too. He only needed to be shown a routine once or twice and he had it fixed in his head. At playtime at school, he would often take himself off, stand in front of a reflective window, and dance. He wasn't bothered he looked a bit odd chatting away to himself. Or that other children were laughing. It made him happy and it was his way of coping with a situation he found stressful.

Playing cricket with his dad was another 'happy place' Jamie would relive over and over again. No matter how many times he bowled the ball, he never got fed up. Even when he missed the stumps ten times in a row.

"*Ty 'gen,*" he would say throwing his arms up in the air in mock disgust, going back to the stumps to try again.

It never failed to amaze me how hard he would try when he wanted to. He was actually really good at bowling, and that takes quite a lot of skill so Cliff tells me.

"*At?*" he would say around the time Cliff would be due home from work. This was usually after we'd eaten dinner – he couldn't tell the time so meal times and other routines often set out the day for him.

"*At, Addy owm Amie,*" he would mutter, repeating what I'd told him that Daddy would play cricket with him when he got home over and over until Cliff walked through the door. At night when he was half-asleep, he babbled under his breath about '*at*' and there was a real contentment in his voice. I think it was about the fact he not only loved cricket, but he was actually good at it and this made him feel great about himself.

When Jamie needed to switch off or wind down, he could find one of his happy places without a problem. It was like flicking a switch. In the doctor's surgery when he had to sit and listen to us talk about the latest results, he would often take himself there. In the middle of the doctor talking blood tests results, he would announce *"at"* or *"Ams show"* and chat away about it to himself. He would zone out of the boring world and tune into somewhere much more fun.

It was so easy for him; sometimes too easy and as he got older I wondered if his happy places were taking over from real life too much.

SELF-TALK

Talking to themselves or 'self-talk' seems to be quite common amongst children and adults with Down syndrome and there have been studies in to why this is. It is nothing to worry about and is often a way for your child or young adult to process the day's events or talk themselves through what they are trying to do.

I have found listening in can be a good way to find out if there are things worrying Jamie as he tends to mutter to himself a lot when there is something bothering him – especially at night before sleep.

However, if your child is a regular self-talker it may be worth encouraging them early on to keep their self-talk to their own private spaces, just to save any awkward situations as they get older. Perhaps suggest a time and place for it if they start talking to themselves when you are out. You could even use a visual prompt – either a sign ('stop' followed by 'later', or a picture of their room for example) or verbal.

Talking to themselves doesn't suggest any mental health issues or delusional tendencies but if it increases in frequency you may want to consider if there is something bothering your child that they may not know how to share with you.

(library.down-syndrome.org/en-us/research-practice/online/2008/parent-carer-ratings-self-talk-behaviour-adults-down-syndrome-canada-united-kingdom)

CHAPTER 15

MISCONCEPTIONS, MISUNDERSTANDINGS

One day, I received a text from a good friend that read:

Today is international disadvantaged people's day.
Please send an encouraging message to a retarded friend,
just as I've done. I don't care if you lick windows, interfere
with farm animals, or occasionally shit yourself.
You hang in there sunshine, you are fxxxxxx special.

When I read it, I was shocked, upset and surprised. I didn't respond to the text – what would I have said? I checked and re-checked the sender details, as I just couldn't believe this particular friend would have sent this to me.

I questioned if I was being too sensitive and scolded myself for not being able to take a joke. When I got home later that day, there was a message from my friend asking me to call her. I also got a text saying how sorry she was, she didn't think, didn't want to offend me and she had been thoughtless.

I responded that I appreciated her apology and I would call her when I could.

It left me feeling very down and with a battle going on in my head.

Had this same text had a racist word in it, would my friend still have sent it? If it had a sexist slant, would she have sent it? No is the simple answer.

How could anyone, let alone anyone who vaguely knew me – or Jamie – think I would find that of all things funny? I knew she truly hadn't thought and immediately realised her mistake and was mortified.

What bothered me the most though was that these kinds of *jokes* existed at all and people we know and love laughed at them. Did they not see the offence it would cause?

When this kind of thing happened, it reminded me because Jamie is a minority he is likely to be treated as a secondary citizen, however wrong this is. People still think it's okay to mimic those who are not quite as smart as others. Children still laugh at the way other children like Jamie talk, jokes are still made about *flids, mongs, spastics* and *retards*. As a school girl, I know I would put my tongue in the bottom of my lips and say, "Duh, are you thick" and didn't think anything of it. It wasn't until I was older I actually understood what I was doing and what my words and actions referred to. By then I'd probably upset countless mums, sisters, brothers just like me.

This kind of acceptance of harmless humour, or whatever it is people like to pretend it is, stretches wide.

Sam had a run-in with a younger boy at school when he was around nine years old. The younger boy was making fun of the way Jamie talked. Sam, ever the protective big brother, heard him and pushed him telling him not to do it. He got in trouble for shoving the boy and came home upset about the whole incident and anxious he was in trouble.

I called the school and asked if I could go in to speak to the head teacher about it. When I met the head the next day in her office she was keen to emphasise to me how they instill in the children the importance of not retaliating. She said Sam, as the older child, should have known better. I listened but thought to myself, *how many nine-year-old boys could keep a cool head in that situation? How many would calmly go and 'tell tales'?*

After the head had given me the full rundown on the school's policy on dealing with children who get in trouble for retaliating, I reminded her perhaps she should also address the issue of children who make fun of those less able than themselves. She finally agreed yes, that shouldn't have happened and next time Sam should tell her immediately. I left the office feeling very frustrated thinking *Err ... no, next time he should shove the kid a bit harder and remind him he's not as smart as he thinks.*

Obviously, I would not really condone this type of retaliation but as a parent it's so hard to listen to those who are responsible for disciplining children miss the point completely.

Having had time to mull over things following the offensive text message, my friend and I chatted on the phone. She was deeply sorry for even considering sending me the message and also said she totally agreed it wasn't a funny joke in the first place. We finished the conversation and I knew our friendship was probably stronger from the frank exchange and I felt better we had been honest with each other about it.

Afterwards, I still worried I had been too sensitive. Was I too quick to frown and too easily upset by what others might view as a harmless joke? Did people worry about what they said around me or were careful about what jokes they told? I hated to think I came across as po-faced and unable to take a joke. Or I was so PC I couldn't take a joke anymore.

This was just something I would have to accept. I know what's correct for me and my family. When is it okay to laugh at someone because of the colour of their skin, their lack of speech, their physical disability or their looks?

Well, never.

Not so sweet

Ask any parent or carer of a child with Down syndrome and they will have heard these comments (or variations of them) on a number of occasions:

"Ah Down's are such loving people, aren't they?"

"Oh, you must get so much love from him/her."

"They are so sociable and friendly."

~

First of all, I have to address the elephant in the room.

People WITH Down syndrome are people first. They HAVE Down syndrome. They are NOT Down syndrome. Woe betide anyone who forgets that around me. It is probably my number one pet hate.

~

The loveable, friendly characteristics our children are attributed with though are slightly skewed and can become more of an issue as our children grow up. What other people view as friendliness is in fact a lack of boundaries and is something we as parents have to teach very early on. Something most children learn naturally can be something our children struggle with. We need those who support, teach or just say hello to our children to also teach it.

When Jamie was a six-year-old for example, he would greet everyone he met with a cheery *"Ello!"* and, as his speech developed would ask, *"Wa's or name?"* determined to find out their name.

This was fine if it was the new boy at school but not so good when it was a teenager queuing behind us at the supermarket checkout.

I explained to Jamie a number of times he didn't need to say hello to everyone he saw, that he shouldn't approach people he didn't know. But it didn't always seem to get through. One evening in particular stands out as a time when this 'friendliness' became a real concern.

This particular night, we were at a presentation evening for Sam's cricket team. Jamie was around seven at the time. Sam was almost ten by now and becoming more independent by the day and was looking forward to being with his friends. Louise, who as a three-year-old toddler loved any excuse to dress up and have a run around, came along too.

The presentation was held in the cricket club just a short walk from our house. Cliff had been playing in the adult team as well as going along to Sam's matches, so he knew a lot of the people going. I hadn't been that involved with the club as I had my hands full looking after Jamie and Louise (who often got bored during matches).

We had been there about an hour when Jamie decided to wander off (he is a 'runner' remember and my guard was probably down as it was a familiar place to us all).

"Have you seen Jamie?" I asked Cliff who was at the bar talking to someone.

"No, I thought he was with you?" his brow furrowed immediately.

"I'll check the club house, you check the toilets." I sprang in to action leaving Sam with Louise. When Cliff and I couldn't find him in the club house or the marquee outside that had been set up for the presentation, we started to panic. A few more people picked up on our panic and sent search parties out in to the playing field and the park outside. As word spread around the club house a shout came up from across the bar.

"It's okay, he's with Mick, in there watching the television!"

Sure enough, as we looked we could see his blonde head among a group of men – watching television. Cliff and I breathed a sigh of relief, as he was safe. However, when we headed over to get him my relief was short-lived. There he was, happily sat on Mick's lap, watching the television, clearly enjoying the general banter within the group.

My immediate thought was: he barely knows this man, neither do I. What if ...

Luckily, Cliff did know the man well enough to know there was nothing to worry about and in that situation, I knew it was all very harmless.

Later that same evening, after the presentation had taken place we decided to leave. Yet again we had to hunt down Jamie *(he's just so slippery; we do watch him like a hawk – honest!)* This time we found him in the middle of a group of people, claiming one of the young boy's trophies as his own.

"Come on, Jamie, we have to go home now. Give the boy his trophy back," I said, reaching for his hand and passing the trophy back to a slightly worried looking boy.

"Say bubye," Jamie said and with that launched himself at the boy's dad, flung his arms round his shoulders and gave him a huge hug. A real cuddle. The man, clearly feeling slightly awkward, laughed it off; "Ah, thanks mate" and gave him a half cuddle back. He then gave him an affectionate kiss on the head.

Feeling a little uncomfortable I literally had to prise Jamie away — spilling the man's drink in the process.

"Oh, I'm so sorry," I said, not a little embarrassed. We left as quickly as we could.

Walking home Cliff could see I wasn't happy and asked what was wrong.

"Didn't you see? Jamie was clambering all over that guy and I didn't want to make a scene, but he can't do that. He has to know it's not always safe. What if we didn't know that man, what if he does that when we're not around to look out for him? Why did he go over to him in the first place?"

"Jo, he was a guy I play cricket with, it's fine, he won't have minded at all. He knows Jamie." Cliff tailed off.

He clearly didn't get it and I was angry he didn't.

"Cliff, what if Jamie does this to a not-so-nice person? Someone who could take advantage of his friendliness. What if he did it to someone who was less tolerant or that felt really uncomfortable with it? We have to teach him it's not appropriate."

We walked the rest of the way home in silence. Both aware Jamie was growing up and we needed to equip him better with the changes this would bring. For a start we had to talk to him about when is it okay to hug a complete stranger.

Help him understand actually it's never okay.

Later that evening I told Cliff about an incident at the trampoline club Jamie was going to. It was a weekly class held in a local sports club specifically for children with various special needs.

"Emily, who started last week, was so excited to come again this week when she arrived she ran in and came straight to me for a hug. I returned the hug, flattered she'd remembered me. But I did feel a bit awkward," I explained to him.

"Her mum came over and told her off for hugging me. I was a bit embarrassed. But she was right. I should have realised this wasn't appropriate at all, I barely know her!"

I wanted Cliff to see my reaction at the cricket club wasn't an overreaction.

"When he was a baby or toddler it was cute when Jamie smiled at strangers in the street, but can't you see, as he grows older, it's not. The smile turns into a stare, turns into him saying hello, then what? Teenage girls do not want boys they don't know randomly talking to them at the park about Barney or trains or whatever." I was getting annoyed as it seemed he just didn't see the problem.

"Not all grown men know how to handle a young boy they've never met throwing their arms around them."

He thought about it for a while and agreed. We needed to consider this problem and maybe should have earlier than now.

"But how do we explain this to Jamie? It's okay for him to speak to people he doesn't know but only if we say it's okay first? It's not okay to talk to strangers randomly in the street but he should be polite to say, Ruth in the post office or the old lady down the road who always asks him how he is?" Cliff was as irate as I was.

I didn't have all the answers, but we both agreed to try to help him understand social boundaries and how they work.

The following day I did some research and found out about the circles curriculum. Annoyingly I couldn't access it at the time as it seemed only to be used in America. However, I gleaned some information from the website and to be honest became quite confused myself. I wondered how Jamie would get it if I couldn't. To understand hugging family was okay, but only close friends should be hugged. How to define close friends? What kind of hug? I knew this would take some time.

The lack of boundaries also showed itself in other ways. At Jamie's seven-year-old height, if he poked someone to get his or her attention it usually ended up being just below waist level. This was not good when it was a man standing in front of him. He would tug on trousers and pat bottoms until he got the person's attention. If someone was sitting down, he would pat them to get their attention. Quite often, this would be women's chests. It was always very awkward and I would try to remind him he should speak to get people's attention, not touch.

As most little (and big) boys do, Jamie liked to explore inside his trousers. Not an issue in itself as it's a perfectly natural thing to do. But teaching him when and where was appropriate was important. Usually a seven-year-old boy would somehow know it is only appropriate to do that kind of thing in private. But with Jamie it was something we had to teach him. We would tell Jamie a hundred times a day to get his hands out of his pants and remind him of privacy. I explained only to do this in his bedroom with the door closed. I constantly used the word 'private' and 'appropriate' so he got used to what it meant.

As with most things, Jamie did learn and by the time he was eight or so he understood this kind of exploration was for his own room only.

As he got older this kind of anti-social or immature behaviour had to be continually addressed. He had to be taught boundaries his peers seemed to learn naturally, and he had to be told what was and wasn't appropriate more often. As with everything else, the learning – and teaching – never stops.

CIRCLES CONCEPT

The Circles Concept, developed by James Stanfield an American-based authority in Special Education and Instructional Design, teaches children how to recognise social boundaries. It is literally a series of coloured circles that parents (or educators) can use to represent people their children know and the appropriate levels of intimacy. It is usually taught within an educational setting but the information is available online and can be downloaded.

You can do something similar yourself by using photos and images of people your child is in contact with. Show your child the photo or picture and ask if s/he should hug, shake hands or simply greet each person. You may be surprised by their response. Explain some people are friends who we touch and friends who we don't touch, that family is okay to hug and so on. IF they are able to cope with more information explain the types of hug you can give – a full on hug for mum and dad, but maybe a side hug for an older cousin.

Be very clear about strangers and what that means (someone they have never met before or don't know very well) are not to be spoken to at all unless you have said they can. If your child is old enough, role play some situations with them. Tell them you are going to pretend to be their head teacher for example and explain the correct way to say hello. Do the same for the guy who delivers the post, their best friend, their sibling etc. Setting boundaries early on will really help in later life.

Also teach body boundaries using realistic images of a male and female body. Explain 'red' areas (where underwear covers as a general rule) are private and only they, you or a medical professional you have given permission to, can touch them there. Give them words or signs they should use if they ever need to. Stop! Don't! Along with hand gestures.

Also explain these areas are where they should not touch other people too. Using the colour red – a colour associated with raised awareness – will trigger their visual memory.

Keep revisiting boundaries with them as their friendship groups grow and their situation changes (starting a new school or moving to a new house for example) and reassess as necessary.

(www.stanfield.com/product/circles-curriculum-bundle-w1037-3)

Helping hands

Emotionally it could be very draining looking after Jamie. He was incredibly demanding at times and this wasn't always because of what *he* was doing. A lot of emotion was spent worrying, thinking, getting angry, being sad and just working things out with Jamie that sometimes there was little left for anybody else. The physical side of things also took its toll. Years of dressing and undressing him, lifting him in to bed when he refused to budge, carrying him if he didn't – or couldn't – walk any more. As he got older (and more determined), this obviously became harder. So sometimes both Cliff and I would be physically and emotionally exhausted.

For this kind of exhaustion, help was hard to find. There was no one to step in and say, *you know what, let us do that for a while*. Not without a lot of paperwork or a dozen phone calls to make. Few people ever wanted to hear how frustrated you were when yet another meeting at school went badly. No one wanted to hear Jamie had wet himself yet again and you really could wring his neck. While family can – and have – helped out when we took a weekend break or a night out, we always felt we were imposing on them. I was also more aware of this as Jamie – and my parents – got older. Things got harder. But my family always stepped up and I'm sure always will. I feel for those people in our situation who don't have family to be there for them. This was brought home to us after we moved to Singapore and were without that lifeline.

Once Jamie started school, Helena, who was by now like one of the family, still continued to be part of his life and would take him swimming every now and then or just take him to Kim and Joe's, her parents. It's people like this that have been so valuable to us in so many ways.

It was the smallest offers of help that made the biggest difference. Someone else taking him out for the afternoon so we could watch Sam play football without having to be on the lookout for Jamie's frequent pitch invasions. Another pair of hands getting him dressed or cleaned up. And more importantly, someone *doing* something *with* Jamie rather than just babysitting him while he watched the television. We needed people who would engage him and help him develop.

When Jamie turned eight, and following a conversation with a friend who also had a child with special needs, I finally decided the time was right to ask the social services once again for help. Around then, direct payments had been introduced for families such as ours to employ a carer-type person for anything from one hour a week. It meant having an assessment to determine how many hours you were entitled to, but my friend had gone through the process and when she told me she had taken all three of her children on a trip to the Science Museum in the summer, I was convinced. Without the extra help, she, like me, could never have considered even trying it. But, with a spare pair of hands and eyes she was able to spend time with all three of her children, with no one missing out.

The 'befriender' as they were known, could be used in different ways, from taking the child to an after-school club or going to the cinema, to staying at home with them while the parent did something for themselves.

After a very lengthy process involving many meetings with our new social worker and a ton of forms to fill in, we were allocated ten hours of help per week. I was amazed and gobsmacked! I was only expecting two, maybe three hours per week at the most. There was a sense of relief; someone else could see that we needed some help. I felt verified.

There was still the issue of finding someone though. I wasn't comfortable asking a stranger to help so the obvious person to ask was Helena. Over the years, she had developed a fantastic relationship with Jamie and although she was now working full time and Jamie was at school, she still kept in touch and saw Jamie.

She had recently changed job, that meant she worked just a short drive away and had some spare time. The fact we could pay her officially helped to dispel some of the guilt I felt.

Once we had agreed what Helena could help with it took me a while to get used to letting go. I felt guilty I wasn't taking Jamie to his drama club. I felt guilty for sending him off with her on a Sunday morning while I went with Cliff to watch Sam play football. I felt even worse when I asked Helena to take Jamie swimming while I spent the morning at home with Lou – especially as Lou made it quite clear she would rather go swimming with Helena too!

But I got used to it. I didn't have to rush around quite so much and I think Sam and Lou enjoyed it too. It did make things easier for a while.

After a year or so Jamie started being less keen to go out with Helena. Not because she had done anything different. He just wasn't enjoying it as much. I think the problem was he was growing up. I could understand that too. How many nine-year-old boys want to hang out with a twenty-five-year-old, no matter how cool they are? Helena was also busier and so I knew it was time to look for an alternative. For the next couple of years, we tried a few other befrienders and some worked better than others. Jamie had made friends with a lovely young man called Sam – or Sam Hammond as we always had to call him. He and Sam often went out together with their befrienders and that worked well. They would go bowling, to the cinema, out for a burger and so on.

This kind of help was priceless and with the social interaction with friends his own age, Jamie finally started to feel he had a social life and was becoming more independent. The importance of this kind of service can't be measured.

But, as a parent, when you are using a service like this, there is the constant worry funding will be cut and help no longer available. Then what do we do?

Asking for help is really hard, getting it is even harder.

CHAPTER 16

I'LL BE THERE FOR YOU

I am lucky I think, as I have many friends. Friends from school, from work, from having children and even from this strange world of writing. I like having friends and without them I wouldn't be the person I am. They mean a lot to me and some of my friends, I feel, are like family.

Various friendships changed after I became a mum. This isn't uncommon, after all becoming a parent is life-changing. But what surprised me more were the friendships that changed because I'm Jamie's mum.

Over the years, even those closest to me haven't always been able to understand what it means to be the parent of a child with special needs. I don't think it has been lack of interest, or they didn't or don't care. Maybe it was lack of knowledge – they simply didn't know what I was dealing with and didn't know how to ask? So, ultimately was it lack of information from me? Did I close up? When I dig deep I think

I can honestly say it's a bit of both. I changed, of course I did. But so did friends.

Some friends gave the impression bringing up Jamie was just like parenting any child, and said as much. For example, if I mentioned Jamie had been up all night, they would recall the last time their child was up, and how difficult it had been. If I talked about Jamie refusing to budge in the middle of the shops, they would agree children were the most awkward buggers sometimes. Of course, everyone had their difficult times; we could all sympathise and empathise with the various obstacles our children seemed to throw our way.

What I felt some friends just didn't understand was these obstacles were often not phases. He wouldn't grow out of them, certainly not very quickly anyway and not without a lot of effort on my part.

There were friends like Nic and Samantha I could be honest with when things were tough and I had been surviving on two hours sleep for a week. There were other friends who just wanted to hear all was okay. With some friends, I would skirt around issues that were either too hard for me to discuss, or I felt they wouldn't really listen or try to understand. Maybe this was unfair; after all, part of a friendship is trust and openness. But I'm sure I am not alone when I say as a parent of a child with special needs, sometimes you daren't open up for fear of them judging you or your child. Or often in my case, you didn't want to say how awful you were feeling or badly you were coping because you knew once you started, you may never stop.

It was hard to accept even those you thought were close friends could not be empathic or even worst, I was embarrassed to be honest around.

Friends have surprised me with their reactions and after one particular incident I became very conscious of how I reacted to awkward situations.

Jamie was around eight years old and along with Sam and Louise we had been invited to a friend's house who had a son a similar age to Sam. Joining us was a really close friend of mine who had two boys, one of whom was the same age as Jamie. For an hour or so, the boys were upstairs playing and all was well. We then decided to go to a park a short drive away, so we all jumped in our own cars to meet there. In the car on the way, Sam seemed a bit quiet.

"You okay, Sam, you're very quiet?" I asked him.

He shook his head and looking at his lap said he wanted to go home.

"But why? I thought you were enjoying yourself?"

"No, I'm not. I just want to go home. Can we go home now? I don't want to go to the park. Nor do you, do you J?" his dark, almond-shaped eyes looked at Jamie as he took his hand in his.

I stopped the car and turned to face him.

"What's up, Sam. Have you and the others had a row?"

"No, Mum, I just want to go home." His dark eyebrows knitted together and he squirmed in his seat.

"Sam, you need to tell me what's going on. We can't just not turn up at the park, the others are expecting us. What's happened?"

"It's them, Josh 'n' Oscar, they're not being very nice. They keep making fun of JJ when he talks and then when we started playing hide and seek Josh said we should run away from Jamie cos he couldn't play it properly. I don't like it." Sam was getting angrier as he spoke and I reached across and stroked his arm.

"I should've told you before shouldn't I? Sorry."

"You don't have to say sorry Sam, you've told me now. Let's just go to the park for a little while then we'll go home I promise. I'll keep a close eye on Jamie don't worry." I tried to reassure him and stay calm. Inside my stomach was doing somersaults. I hated any kind of confrontation and I really didn't know what I would say to my two friends about the way their children had behaved.

In the ten minutes or so it took to drive to the park a hundred things went through my head. I had noticed Jamie was lagging behind when this particular group were playing, but had hoped this was his choice rather than he was being left out. It was impossible to police his playing all the time – but I felt guilty I hadn't noticed anything wrong. But, I reasoned, not everyone wants to be friends with Jamie and that should be their choice.

Whichever way I looked at it I had to speak to my friend about it straight away. I was feeling very angry and upset and on reflection maybe I should have waited to discuss the problem when I was a little less emotional. But I didn't. As soon as the boys were off playing I told them what Sam had said about their boys making fun of Jamie and leaving him out. Apparently, I said it in a very direct, confrontational way. Honestly, I don't know if I was too angry or not angry enough, I just blurted it out and tried not to cry.

Josh's mum refused to believe he would have done that. Both women outrightly said I was being oversensitive and critical of their children. One of them then pointed out surely I realised this kind of thing probably went on at school all the time. That Jamie would be made fun of and left out of games. At this point, I realised they both thought I was overreacting and maybe even Sam was lying. I left (as quickly as you can when you've got three children in tow) very angry and upset and with the feeling my 'friends' thought I was somehow making this up and being oversensitive.

We were all very quiet on the way home and I tried to reassure Sam he'd done the right thing. Once again I was proud of not only his loyalty to his brother, but his strong sense of right and wrong.

To this day I have no idea what my so-called friend meant by her comment about this happening elsewhere. *So what? I should get used to it? That he didn't mind? That I shouldn't? That it was a fact of life?*

Later that day I called Oscar's mum to talk about what had happened. She was, after all, a very good friend and I didn't want this to ruin our friendship. At first, she ignored my calls (this was before text messaging, Facebook and the like, so it was much easier to ignore people).

Eventually, after trying her number two or three times she answered. I told her what Sam had told me and why I was upset. She listened to me but disagreed the boys had been anything but friendly to Jamie. She cited times when 'allowances' had been made for Jamie; about the times Jamie would hug her younger son too hard and knock him over. Also, times Jamie had hit one of the boys or been heavy handed in some way. They said at times like that they could have confronted me about it but chose not to as they knew it wasn't 'his fault'. But now he was older, it wasn't acceptable and they would not put up with it. We went around in circles for a while until I realised we weren't going to understand each other. We ended the conversation with no mention of when we'd be in touch again.

Once off the phone I thought about what my friend had said. I tried to see it from her point of view. Yes, he could definitely be heavy handed sometimes and would bowl into people unable to stop himself. If that person was a little person, they would invariably get knocked over. Yes, he would swing a bat around without a care in the world, and when he did I'd reprimand him and take the bat away. But he had never, to my knowledge, hurt anyone on purpose. I knew he could go in hard for a kiss sometimes and I tried to remind him it wasn't appropriate. But it was a learning curve for me too and I didn't always get it right.

I had taken for granted as we were friends they understood this. Maybe I should have explained things better. I hated it when Jamie knocked Louise over or squeezed her so hard she yelped, but I knew it was never his intention to hurt her. I assumed my friends realised the same. I was so hurt she had chosen to compare her son's meanness to Jamie's lack of awareness about his own strength and his lack of coordination.

It took us a long while to meet up again and when we did it was never the same. I probably wasn't the easiest friend to have as I don't think I ever forgave them for not being more understanding. I guess it was inevitable we'd drift apart. For me it was a friendship I truly treasured, but a few years later – and in that time, we didn't see each other nearly as much – we stopped contacting each other altogether. Well, the truth is they stopped contacting me.

When I think about that day now it still stings. Losing that friendship was one of the hardest things I've dealt with and still bothers me. Looking back, I wonder if I could have handled it better; but I did what I thought was right at the time. I've often wondered if they have ever regretted their words or if they ever spoke to their children about their words and actions.

Too much information?

As Jamie grew older, some issues were definitely more uncomfortable to deal with and I became very adept at glossing over things or not letting friends know the full story.

One such time we had Nic, Mark, Samantha and Mike round for dinner. As we sat down for dinner, Louise was tucked up in bed, Sam was in his room but Jamie was still wide awake – no surprise to any of us – so we left him dancing to his videos in the living room.

The dining room opened on to the living room and from where I was sitting I could see what he was up to. During dinner, he went a little quiet. Call it mother's instinct but I looked over and saw him kicking something on the floor.

"What's that you're kicking Jamie?" A classic example of putting mouth into action before brain, I knew before I'd even finished asking that there had been a 'toilet incident' and it obviously hadn't stayed in his night pants (we didn't say nappy now he was older).

Oblivious to poo protocol, he looked at me, promptly picked it up, walked over to me and handed me his 'prize'. Honestly, I should have been a sleight of hand magician as it was in my napkin before anyone noticed what it was. I then – without making eye contact with anyone else – looked directly at Cliff who read 'the look' immediately (a skill we'd honed). With no fuss, he left the table and whisked Jamie to the bathroom to clean him up saying: "come on Jamie, come with Daddy."

"Everything okay, Jo? Can we do anything?" Nic asked.

"No, it's okay, he just needs a wee, I'll just check Cliff reminds him to brush his teeth while he's there," I rolled my eyes in a 'what do you do with him' kind of way and told them to carry on with dinner as I whisked the napkin well out of smelling range.

I did a quick recce of the living-room floor, just to check there were no other surprises lurking around, went to Jamie's room and grabbed a clean pair of pyjamas and took them to the bathroom. Cliff was giving Jamie a shower as he was in a bit of a mess and I could see he now needed a clean shirt too. I ran to our room, got the clean shirt, took it to Cliff and we then both returned to the table with a freshly showered Jamie deposited back on the sofa and given strict instructions to sit down and not move.

This all took no more than ten minutes. Samantha asked if Jamie was okay. They seemed to have come to the conclusion Jamie had wet himself. They all recounted times their children had wet themselves – with stories of them being too excited by grandad's story to get up and go to the loo or jumping too vigorously on the trampoline. The atmosphere was relaxed, and I really didn't see the point of explaining it was a bit more than a wee, and it was actually becoming a regular occurrence. That I was sick of being on poo watch and really, when was this stage going to end? Not because I was embarrassed or felt our friends would be unsympathetic – in fact, quite the opposite. It was just it wasn't necessary; sometimes I just didn't want to go into details. The evening carried on and we had a lovely time.

Another time I recall, two other friends who each had two-year-old boys, were discussing what a pain it was their boys were still in nappies at night. They asked me what advice I had – obviously thinking, as two of my children were older, I could help. They were oblivious to the fact Jamie, at six years old, was still wearing night pants. I swerved the question by saying Sam still wore a night nappy around two, they shouldn't worry and each child was different. Their boys would do it in their own time. On that occasion, I was embarrassed to admit Jamie was still wearing night pants and I felt it would be difficult to be honest about this.

Different friends. Different feelings.

When Jamie was younger I didn't want people to feel sorry for us. I hated the idea anyone felt it had been a hardship having

Jamie. It hadn't. It was just a bit tough sometimes. While I wanted to share worries and concerns, I didn't want to bombard them so they thought it was all hard work. Sometimes it felt like I had no one to talk to who really understood. But then a friend would come up trumps, see I was struggling, and help, either with words or actions. Or I would turn to friends who had children with Down syndrome too and they would reassure me with familiar stories and helpful advice.

For me, friends are invaluable and like all relationships take a bit of work. Some I have worked harder at than others, some have – and will – change over time. That's life and I believe you have to know when to let go.

Balance is what is needed. Friends come in all shapes and sizes, with all types of needs and expectations of each other. How I've changed since becoming Jamie's mum may not be what some of my old friends expected or needed. That's okay; we move on. Other friends have shown their worth a hundred times over by thoughts and gesture and by just being there. This has deepened our friendship more than I could have hoped for. New friends have become invaluable and will, I hope, remain that way.

I know how important friendships are to me and would like for all of my children to have good friends they can trust. I want them to know how to make a friendship work and I want them to know friends can come and go. Some may even stay for the duration. Those are the ones you want around during the tough times.

CHAPTER 17

REFLECTIONS

Cliff's job was increasingly taking him to Singapore, usually for a week at a time every six months or so; this would be on top of all the other travelling he did to various places in between. When he went away for work it was always hard on me as it left me pretty much as a single parent. Luckily my family were on hand to help out if I needed them to sit with Louise while I went to see Sam's teacher or took Jamie to his trampoline club. After a while, Cliff travelling away became something I was used to.

My younger sister by now had two girls of her own, Talia who was born fifteen months before Louise, and Tilly who came along fifteen months after. Louise loved to spend time with them, as did Jamie. It wasn't unusual for all four of them to pile round to my parents' house, play dress up and put on endless shows. Jamie had no qualms about being bossed around by his little sister and cousins and would tolerate endless demands like "come on Jamie, you introduce us" and would proudly stand in front of his never-bored Nanna and Grandad declaring, *"an here are tars of show, eese, taya, teeyee"* gesturing to the three girls who'd be standing to the side in their mismatch of clothes that Mum kept in the 'special dressing-up box' she kept.

As Jamie introduced the 'stars of the show' my dad would always clap along enthusiastically. This would lead to Jamie taking longer than his allocated time, showing off his dance moves to sounds of Louise impatiently shouting "Jaymeeeee, come on it's our turn!" and Nanna cheering him. Poor Mum and Dad would have to sit for hours watching them all and never once hurried them along. Sometimes they'd even rope Sam in who'd fake reluctance but end up singing or doing a little number with them. On special occasions, like Christmas, they'd all try their best to get Jake – my eldest sister Michelle's son – to join in. But being a good ten years older than them he was happier to watch and clap along. The shows became part of the family get-togethers.

When Louise was around two-and-a-half the opportunity came up during the Easter holidays for us all to go to Singapore *with* Cliff. We of course jumped at the chance. The idea was although Cliff would be working during the day, we could spend time together in the evenings. It would at least mean Cliff would be in the same country as us and, of course, gave me and the kids a great opportunity to relax and have a holiday.

We all had a great time, spending our days at the hotel pool or visiting the Merlion, butterfly park and zoo. At the hotel, Sam, although shy in some ways, seemed to attract people to him and once the initial awkwardness was out of the way, he'd happily include whoever wanted to play in his games around the pool. Louise loved the fact she could be in the water all day long and she and Jamie spent hours chasing up and down the slide together, with Sam keeping them company in between games. In the evening, they all loved getting dressed up ready for dinner with Daddy when he got 'home'. It was then that I think we all fell a little bit in love with the Lion City with its smell of lemongrass and satay, city lights and the constant buzz of traffic.

That first trip to Singapore also gave me an opportunity to reflect. I don't know if it was something to do with a book I was reading at the time – *Blue Sky July*, a fabulous book about a mother, Nia Wynn, whose son has cerebral palsy – or maybe it was the stage/age Jamie was at. I remember thinking a lot on that holiday about how much Jamie had changed. In particular, one simple thing led me to consider how far we'd come.

I was in the hotel room early evening, reading my book having spent the day around the pool with the kids. Jamie came into me giggling, with both his legs inside one leg of his shorts. His impish smile and infectious laugh pulled at my heart and I realised he had taken himself to the loo and got in a bit of a pickle. This funny mishap reminded me how far he had come in seven short years.

He had known he needed a wee, taken himself, got muddled with his shorts, seen the funny side and waddled in to get help AND camped up the funny side. Before then, he would either have asked me to take him or having taken himself, got frustrated when he couldn't get his shorts on right and got upset with himself for getting it wrong.

Feeling a bit emotional after reading the book, I helped him sort his shorts out and pulled him to me. I told him – for the millionth time – how clever he was, and truly meant it. With Lou having a nap and Sam downstairs in the games room, I wanted to make the most of our time alone so I asked him to play Snap:

"No!", he said quite determinedly; he was watching his second *Barney* DVD of the day. I tried to persuade him by asking if he wanted to play something else.

"No want to, watching, Barney!" he said shaking his head.

So, I relented, much quicker than I would have had a year or so ago. I'd learned to accept his love of television. As he turned around and headed back to his much-loved Barney, still giggling to himself, I considered how lucky we were.

Later on in the holiday I was reminded once again how much Jamie had grown. He had been communicating what he wanted quite clearly and made it clear he wanted to do things on his own. As I watched him climb the difficult steps to the water slide, I saw just how like the other kids he was. Up and down the slide, in the pool for hours, splashing around. When he went out on a kayak with the other kids in the kids' club, I was so proud. He had made friends too. I know the lady who worked there had a lot to do with his being accepted within the group. There were no questions about what Jamie could and couldn't do, no pages of forms to fill out and not having to fork out for a babysitter because the 'club had regulations'. However, it was also Jamie's confidence in himself that helped.

There were also glimpses of Jamie at his most awkward that reminded me we were not out of the woods yet. One day I had to literally drag him around Singapore Zoo. It was swelteringly hot and before we had left he was asking to watch *Barney*. He wasn't interested in the amazing animals. He just wanted to watch television. By the end of that day, me, Louise and Sam were all feeling miserable because Jamie had been such hard work. His sitting down stunts led me to consider donating him to the zoo as a perfect specimen of English wildlife. But we made it through the day and can laugh now.

Another incident on that same holiday has a place in family history as one of the scariest and funniest 'Jamie incidents'.

I had been in the hotel room, sitting on the patio reading. In the room, a mere five feet away, Jamie was having his *Barney* fix while everyone else was out. The room door was double locked and as usual I had one ear open for him the whole time. After a short while I heard a knock at the door. It was only once I went to answer the door did I realise Jamie wasn't actually in the room and the DVD was playing to itself.

Calling his name and beginning to panic slightly, I opened the door in a rush – and there stood Jamie, in his pants and socks, holding the maid's hand, looking very pleased with himself, grinning. In broken English and with lots of gesturing, the maid told me she had found Jamie wandering around the lobby, heading towards the pool. Luckily, the maid was quick thinking and steered Jamie back to our room.

I thanked the maid profusely and shooed Jamie in to the room.

God forbid he had made it. I hadn't even realised he had left the room!

The door had been double locked and I was checking on him every few minutes. How the hell did he sneak out without me hearing him?

I tried telling him off, explained how dangerous it was, but he seemed pretty nonplussed. I think, in his mind, he'd had enough of *Barney* and wanted to find something else to do. Why tell me?

All kinds of 'what ifs' ran through my mind that night.

What if he had gone to the pool?

What if he had got into the lift?

What if he had met someone who wasn't very nice?

What if he tried to go outside?

But once I'd told him off and tied him to the bed – *joking!* – I laughed. As I calmed down, I laughed a bit more. Imagining the scene, with the maid earlier …

Jamie, wandering around the corridor of the hotel.
In his pants and socks.
Probably singing a Barney song.
Probably stopping to have a dance.
Probably saying hello to everyone he saw.

I wonder if he'll be doing that at fourteen?

Overall, I could see Jamie was growing up. That things were changing slightly. Hopefully getting steadier, if not, dare I imagine, easier?

CHAPTER 18

HOUSTON, WE HAVE A PROBLEM …

But back to school …

With Jamie seeming unhappy at school at the end of Year 2 I was worried as he began Year 3. It was the first year of key stage 2 and I knew from when Sam was in that year that the pressure is steadily increased. The work tends to go up a gear and I wondered how Jamie was going to cope with this and, more importantly, how was the school going to help.

His new teacher had no experience of teaching children with Down syndrome so at the end of the summer term I had given her some background information and suggested websites she might like to look at and so on. It was obvious after our first introduction meeting in that first week she had not read any of the information. She told me she would see how Jamie got on before looking at new ways to work with him. He had a new SA working with him in the afternoons, but luckily still had the same SA in the morning from the previous year.

The first term went along quietly. Jamie wasn't particularly keen on school still but went in and seemed to be coping with things. Over the summer he'd made real progress with his swimming and we or Helena would take him swimming most weekends. He had a funny way of swimming just below the surface of the water and in deep water was still happier wearing arm bands. But it was something he was really enjoying, along with his cricket. All of these things we'd write in his communication book hoping he could talk about it in school and we encouraged him to sign as much as possible. His SA was fantastic at signing with him and anything she didn't understand, she would check with me and we'd work out what he had been trying to say. She really understood the need to give Jamie confidence in his talking.

By this stage I had qualified as a Signalong tutor myself. Having seen the huge benefits of using sign language and with my career as a journalist on hold I had come to the conclusion that teaching Signalong would offer me a challenge and give me something outside of being a mum to concentrate on. So, one week over the summer, I had taken myself off for a week's intensive training course at Signalong's head office in Rochester in Kent, leaving Cliff in charge of the kids (with a fair bit of help from my mum and dad).

It was a really intense course and hard work and was the first time in years I'd been in a learning situation. Having to stand up and 'present' was petrifying but necessary and I came home with a huge sense of achievement – and I passed! I then went on to run courses for parents, teaching staff and even went in to school to teach the children once a week. I loved it and I knew how much it would help future 'Jamies' in the school.

A key point I always made whenever I taught a course was that the adult should always take the blame for not understanding the child. Some of the frustration children with communication difficulties face is lack of patience and understanding from others. They should always praise the child for trying and do everything they can to work out what it is the child is trying to communicate. Be that being led by the hand around the school until they find what they are referring to or asking parents and caregivers if they could help. Either way, they should always go back to the child and tell them they'd found out or although they'd tried their best they were unable to and to say a simple sorry.

Towards the end of that first term I was asked to go in for an IEP (Individual Education Plan) meeting with his teacher. I expected nothing more than the usual chat about goals for the term and what he had achieved and what was next on the list. I was not in any way prepared for the conversation that actually took place. Although I can't remember the exact wording, the conversation went along these lines: "I'm sorry to say Jamie is spending most of his playtime on his own. He isn't really playing with any of his classmates."

"Oh? Do his classmates try to include him in their games? Do you ever ask him why he's not playing with them? Who is supervising him and how do they try to encourage him?" The questions came spilling out of my mouth as I desperately hoped he wasn't sad and lost every playtime.

"Yes, his SA does try to encourage him. He just doesn't seem to want to join in with his classmates," his teacher replied.

She then went on to tell me about a local special needs school she had heard about and how fantastic its resources were.

"Have you ever considered a school like this for Jamie? Maybe he would be better suited there?"

I was stumped. I didn't know how I was meant to respond to this. I felt we were being told our time was up. I told the teacher I would talk to my husband and we'd be in touch.

When I got home I was upset. Of course we had thought about special needs school, what a silly question to ask me. Cliff and I had always said, if and when the time was right.

I phoned Cliff and told him about the conversation.

"Why haven't we noticed something? Why haven't the school been more honest about how Jamie was struggling? Should we start making plans to move him? I feel she is telling us Jamie should leave."

"I can't believe this." Cliff was also in shock "We've told them time and time again to talk to us if they feel there are any problems. I'm going to call the school, Jo, we can't leave it like this. I'll call you back."

Ten minutes later he called back having spoken to the head teacher who had assured him I had got the wrong end of the stick. She said no one was suggesting Jamie should leave mainstream.

"Maybe we've put two and two together and come up with five? Let's just keep an eye on things," Cliff said.

Had I? I replayed the meeting again in my head. Had I misunderstood her?

Alarm bells were ringing.

Things came to a head a month or so later and the situation became very thorny. Jamie's teacher had a problem with Geraldine coming into school. Through comments in his communication book she said she thought Geraldine's over familiarity with Jamie was inappropriate and even suggested we weren't getting value for our money from the speech therapy he was having. His SA also relayed messages from the teacher to us. It got so picky over the weeks the teacher started to tell us if Geraldine was five minutes late and stopped allowing her to use schoolbooks during their sessions.

Geraldine had picked up on the fact Jamie was unhappy. She was very adept at not taking things personally and despite the obstacles being put in front of her, continued to go in to school to work with Jamie. We spoke about it over the phone.

"I wonder if part of his reluctance is actually based on how he feels about himself there? I wonder if he can feel the school just doesn't want him there. Not because they didn't want HIM. They are just not coping with his needs." Geraldine said this gently to me as she knew it would be hard to hear.

She went on to explain she believed if the staff were unsure and/or lacking confidence Jamie was in the right place, he would pick up on it too. When she pointed it out I could see that could be what was happening. His class teacher for example was disappointed he wasn't progressing as she had wanted and expected him to. He felt her disappointment.

With the already growing mountain of paperwork teachers have to deal with, I did understand how the prospect of more wasn't welcomed. Sadly, with Jamie came more paperwork – IEPs, statement assessments, communication books. I could see the extra work was probably the last thing any teacher needed. Also, I couldn't help but think if teachers had really wanted to teach children with special needs they would have specialised. Maybe foisting Jamie on mainstream just wasn't 'fair'.

This is what it had come down to for us now Jamie was in Year 3. The feeling we – and, more importantly, Jamie – got, was it was an obligation. They were trying to educate Jamie because they had to, not because they wanted to. They had stopped trying.

The staff who did go that extra mile were paid back in dividends – his SA last year who had got Jamie writing letters after me and other staff had failed, was bursting with pride for him. What she did involved some creativity and thinking outside the box. She didn't stick to the same old ideas, she tried something new. And it worked! But this initiative stopped as soon as she left. Another SA tuned into Jamie's love of dancing and playing ball. If he was flagging, she would take him out of the class and get him moving – they were often seen dancing to one of the latest chart hits in the computer room.

But this meant those working with him had to go the extra mile too. They had to want to, had to see it was worth it; if not, he just became a burden. Was Jamie beginning to feel this. Feel out of place? A square peg? Was this why he was reluctant to play with his peers, choosing instead to play with the younger children? It broke my heart to think he had begun to realise he was 'different'.

Taking the plunge

That following week, after many discussions, Cliff and I decided to go and visit the local special needs school, Treetops. It had recently been relocated to new, purpose-built premises and we had heard a lot about the facilities there.

Having made an appointment, Cliff and I went along to see for ourselves. We sat nervously in the very modern reception watching a large screen on the wall which showed some of the children who attended the school and boasted about their achievements. The head teacher, Mr Smith, a tall, thin man with greying dark hair came out and greeted us with an open nature that immediately put us at ease. He took us on a tour of the school, showing us around with pride. He loved his job. You could tell.

He talked to most of the children we passed: "Alright Jack, how are you? Did you see the game this weekend, what a shame eh?" he joked with a young boy who looked around fourteen.

As we were shown in and out of state-of-the-art classrooms with huge interactive white boards, colourful examples of the children's work on the walls and spacious timeout areas, all we saw were happy faces – on the staff and students.

We were blown away. More specifically, Cliff was.

"I really thought it would be noisier, more chaotic. I thought we'd see children running around," he whispered to me as we waited while Mr Smith spoke to a child who was clearly meant to be in his classroom.

"Why? What were you expecting. A zoo?" I laughed, relieved he was getting the same feeling about the school as I was.

The whole place gave us the feeling this could be somewhere Jamie would be happy and could flourish. Somewhere he would feel he fitted in.

After seeing the whole school and meeting lots of teachers, Mr Smith showed us out. "Thanks for coming. We'd love to see you come back and next time bring Jamie. We always welcome West Ham fans here!" he shook our hands warmly and laughed.

We both left feeling a buzz of excitement. All the children we saw – with varying special needs – were obviously happy and content at school. It was clear they were pushed to achieve their best and expectations were high. The way they were being taught suited them.

I think we made our decision before we even left the school gates.

It was a couple of weeks before we made a firm decision to take Jamie out of mainstream.

We thought it was our decision to make. Silly us!

CHAPTER 19

TIME FOR CHANGE

When you have a child with Down syndrome in the UK, in our experience, you are pretty much told mainstream school is best for them. For years, the government has been pushing for inclusion and so have encouraged parents like us to put our children into mainstream. We are told, with support, there is no reason our children shouldn't do well in mainstream school. The schools are then pushed to accept children with varying special needs and more often than not, learn on their feet.

The LEA (local education authority) issue statements, staff are supposed to be trained (albeit loosely) and children learn to accept differences among their classmates.

This is all well and good in theory.

What the LEA and the government fail to grasp is this only works if they are willing to spend time and money educating the school and the staff on what this means to them and how to do it.

There's no point pretending. Extra time will be needed. More care will be necessary to help the child. Employing the right person is essential. Training and understanding is vital. Unfortunately, schools are not offered half of this and as a result our children are left floundering.

This was evident to me some years ago when I attended a course called 'Educating Children with Down's in Mainstream School' at Down Syndrome Education International (then known as the Down's Education Trust). It was open to parents, teachers and support staff. I was the only parent on the course at the time. The overwhelming feeling from the other women attending the course was that of slight resentment, of being 'put out' by the children they were working with. These children were just another problem they had to deal with. They meant another extra load of paperwork. Another obstacle to get over.

None of these teachers or support staff spoke badly of the children they were teaching or supporting, it was just a general 'sigh' almost. They weren't bad teachers or SAs. But they didn't choose to teach or help a child with Down syndrome. They were given this extra responsibility as it were, without choice.

It was this difference we saw at Treetops School when we visited. The staff working there knew what they were getting into. More than that, they wanted to work with children with special needs and were supported in doing so. Many were also qualified specifically in areas to do with special needs and so knew how to differentiate work to help the child. If the teacher felt the students needed help understanding the concept of money, they could take them out to the shops and get them using it. If (like Jamie) the idea of words such as 'over', 'under', 'in' and 'out' were still confusing, they could take them into the soft play room and make them physically aware of these prepositions.

It was becoming more obvious to me with inclusion came sacrifice. Our children need to be taught in a different way – they learn differently. And mainstream schools were just not allowed, or not able, to think outside the box.

But it CAN work though. I knew some parents whose children with Down syndrome attended mainstream and flourished. Holly coped well at her local mainstream school and although Karen had to keep on top of things, she was always sure this was the best place for her. I talked at length with Karen about what Holly did, how her SA worked with her and so on. It was clearly working. The school wanted it too.

I also spoke to other parents who had children with special needs and began to see how the smallest things could make a big difference. I was attending a coffee morning at a local support group I joined called SNAP (Special Needs and Parents). I had joined SNAP when Jamie was a toddler and still went along with Louise to the odd coffee morning as it was a great resource. The right supervision at playtime, all of the other children being spoken to about what having special needs means, SAs who differentiate the work so the child could access it and learn.

At the coffee morning, I told some of the mums about our plans to move Jamie to Treetops.

"You know there's a huge waiting list though, don't you?" said Kate whose child was also struggling at mainstream school.

"When I asked about Lewis, they said as we were out of the area getting him there and back might be an issue." This from another mum whose child was also unhappy at mainstream school.

"Yes, you know Julie with Jake had to go to tribunal to get funding for the transport to his new school?" said another parent.

"Of course, you've got to get his current school to agree too. They're not going to want him to leave, are they?" Kate said.

This last comment really caught me by surprise.

"What do you mean? Surely if they're finding Jamie hard to manage, they'll welcome us leaving? Anyway, it's our decision, isn't it?" I asked, suddenly concerned by my lack of knowledge.

"No, sadly not. It's up to the LEA. You have to prove the school are not meeting his needs. They may prefer him to stay as they need the extra money, or have to keep their quota of SN up. Ah, you just never know," Kate said, sighing. It seemed she had done her research.

I wasn't sure. Surely a school's reason for retaining a child could not be mercenary? Could it?

Into battle

That evening I told Cliff about the conversation with the women at SNAP.

"We've made the decision to move Jamie and that's it," Cliff said adamantly, frustration crinkling his hazel eyes.

"We will do whatever we have to get him in to Treetops. But we clearly need to speak to the school sooner rather than later."

The ideal opportunity arose soon after at Jamie's annual review. The night before the review we sat and wrote down every single reason why we felt Jamie's needs weren't being met at mainstream. From lack of training and understanding, to the recent toilet accidents that were an obvious sign of stress. The list was fairly, and worryingly, long. But it needed to be, we were expecting a fight. From what the parents at SNAP had said, for the school to admit they were not meeting Jamie's needs was not something they would do easily.

Cliff was coming along to the meeting too.

"Cliff, can you take the lead today. I really don't think I can speak without becoming emotional – or angry," I said to him as we got ready to leave that morning.

"Okay, but you know I won't beat around the bush. They have to know they're failing him. I'm not going to pretty it up for their feelings." Cliff, as usual, didn't care in this kind of situation if he was going to be liked or not. He just wanted the right result for us – and Jamie. With his by now grey-speckled hair neatly brushed and dressed in a dark suit ready to go straight in to the office afterwards, he cut an impressive figure. I was confident he would know what to say.

At the school, we were shown in to the head teacher's office; a large bland room with a desk at one end and a small cube sofa and round table at the other. Around the table had been placed some chairs clearly taken from a classroom and Cliff and I perched on them and waited for Jamie's teacher and his two SAs to join us which they did shortly after. The head teacher noted down who was there and made formal introductions before starting the meeting. She started to go through the statement, highlighting areas of concern and talking about goals that had been met and areas that might need improvement. She asked how we felt about how Jamie was doing and Cliff asked if he could speak.

"I'm sure you are all aware Jamie has been unhappy at school for a while now. This is obviously a worry for us. We are also concerned with his lack of progress recently. But what really concerns us is he is choosing not to play with his classmates at playtime." Cliff's calm voice held the audience and I kept my head down, looking at my hands.

"We're worried about what this means. You see, we wonder. Is Jamie now noticing he is different?" Cliff voice cracked as he finished the last sentence and then went quiet. So quiet I looked up. Tears were falling down his face. He tried to carry on but couldn't.

This man who until that point had been the strong one in our 'fights' for Jamie gave into feelings that must have been pent up for some time. He covered his face and apologised.

Nobody knew what to say or do and instead everyone looked away.

"Could you please give us a minute?" I asked hastily and they got up and left the room.

Once they left Cliff was immediately embarrassed.

"God. I've no idea where that came from. I'm sorry. I was NOT expecting that. I have no idea what happened then. Sorry, Jo, that didn't quite go to plan did it?" Shoulders drooped in defeat, he bowed his head.

"Don't be silly. You don't have to apologise. I knew I wouldn't get through it without crying. That's why I asked you to talk today. It's shit. What we're having to say is shit. We shouldn't be in this position. Us telling them that he's not feeling like he fits in. It's all so wrong. Please don't apologise." I reached for his hand.

I understood completely and felt awful that I hadn't realised how tough this was for him too. It was admitting aloud Jamie was sad, Jamie could feel the difference now and it bothered him. In some ways, it was admitting we were wrong.

After Cliff and I had gathered ourselves everyone came back in and we resumed the meeting. There was immediately a sense of a weight being lifted. The head teacher told us they would do whatever was necessary to support our decision and they understood it was not personal. They would agree, as a school, they could no longer meet Jamie's needs. I'm not sure if Cliff's display of emotion made a difference. He thinks not. We both feel they had been waiting for us to make the first move.

So that was it. The decision was made. Again, silly us!

ANNUAL REVIEW (BASED ON UK SYSTEM)

At least once a year, the statement or EHCP must be reviewed to see if it is still required or needs updating (amending). The relevant school staff (SENCO, teacher, SA) should attend and the review will focus on the progress your child is making towards the outcomes identified in their EHCP. You – and your child if appropriate – will have an opportunity to talk about how you feel the year has gone. Your child will be supported to take part in the review. From the age of fourteen young people's review meetings will focus on transition and preparation for adulthood and independent living.

After the meeting, a report of what happened will be prepared and circulated to everyone who attended or provided information. Your child's EHCP will then be reviewed based on the meeting and the LEA must let you know their decision within four weeks of the meeting. The decision may be to:

- leave the EHC plan alone
- amend the EHC plan
- cease the EHC plan if it is felt it is no longer necessary for it to be in place

If you are unhappy with the decision, you can discuss this with your SEN Casework Officer.

Fighting our corner

I rang the Local Education Authority (LEA) the next day and spoke to the lady in charge of Jamie's case. I told her we were applying for a place at another school

"It is not as simple as that," she replied tersely, sighing as if she had better things to do. "We will send someone into school to assess the situation and then tell you if *we* agree the move or not. Before anything else we will need to see if there is a way the school could be supporting your son more. I'm afraid it is not up to you to pick and choose." She made it clear she wasn't interested in extending the conversation.

"How long will this take?" I asked, determined not to be fobbed off.

"Not sure. You do know Treetops is full, don't you? The waiting list goes through until 2013. The earliest you can expect to get a place would be 2010." I swear she said this with a fair bit of smugness in her voice.

"Well, it's clear he's not coping and nor are the school. Either he gets a place or I'll have to consider homeschooling him, won't I?" I said with more determination than I actually felt.

Homeschooling? What was I saying? We'd never discussed this, well not seriously anyway. But I felt so desperate I wanted her to know how bad things were for Jamie. We couldn't wait eighteen months! This was so depressing to hear. None of the people at the LEA had even met Jamie, no one had spoken to us about our feelings or asked if he was happy at school. He was just another name on another list.

Mr Smith at Treetops was more helpful. He and Cliff spoke a lot over the next week and for some reason Cliff was positive Jamie would get a place in the next school year. The next month was the end of the Christmas term and Jamie and I were invited by Mr Smith to the school production of *Joseph and his Amazing Technicolour Dreamcoat*. The school hall was packed and it was a great show. Jamie thoroughly enjoyed himself, clapping and joining in with everyone else. After the show Mrs B, who by chance had worked with him previously in mainstream, was the teacher of the class he would go in to. She called us over and introduced him to some of the children.

"Jo, this would be a great school for him. He would absolutely flourish," she told me, clearly loving her job at the school.

"I was told the waiting list is four years long, I'm not sure he'll even be considered yet," I confided.

"Oh, if he's meant to be here, Mr Smith will find a way. Don't worry. Keep pushing, keep fighting. You'll get there."

I wish I felt as confident as she did. Each time we spoke to anyone at the school it was a positive experience. In fact, it made things worse as we felt frustrated. We were kicking ourselves for not considering moving him earlier. If we had moved him the year before he would have been given priority as he was in transition year (infants to juniors).

So, it became a waiting game. I rang the LEA a lot, I made sure the school knew to be totally honest when questioned by LEA. I also reiterated if a place wasn't made available I would be removing Jamie from school and homeschooling him – an idea that filled me with dread in reality.

The last day of the Christmas term, Cliff rang me at work. At the time, I was running a playgroup in the village hall where, a few times a week, local parents and toddlers came and basically ran riot. It was great fun and filled a gap for me as I missed working. It fitted in around the kids. I could take

Louise with me who by now was three years old and loved the fact her mum ran a playgroup. Her playschool was just down the road so on the mornings she was there it was very easy to take and collect her. It was also a nice way to stay part of the village community. I'd opened a special sensory group to cater to young babies with special needs and loved the feedback I got from it. All the sessions included singing and signing time which all the children and parents enjoyed.

My mum (who helped me out running the group), Louise and I had got to the hall early to get it ready for the Christmas party. It was our last day too so I had a lot on organising the party and then packing up for the holidays.

"Just rang to see how you're feeling," Cliff asked – I had been unwell all week with a heavy cold.

"I'm alright, be glad when the party is done to be honest. Now I really have to go."

I was a little impatient as I was trying to get ready for the party and he was acting like he had all the time in the world to chat.

"Ah hang on before you go. I've got something that'll make you feel much better."

I could hear him smiling over the phone and immediately stopped what I was doing.

"Mr Smith has just rung me. Jamie has a place. He can start after Christmas!"

"Why? What? How? When?" a million questions came and went as I immediately started crying.

My mum, came rushing over and, despite the tears, knew straight away it was good news. She hugged me and clapped and cheered knowing how stressful the whole situation had been. Louise, who had looked very concerned at seeing mummy upset, joined in the clapping and did a little dance twirling around in her party dress.

Cliff explained as much as he knew – Mr Smith had been in touch with the LEA and now Jamie had a place. They *wanted* Jamie at their school.

The sense of relief was amazing. I cried, then worried, then questioned, then cried again. The rest of that morning was a blur. In that kind of environment, it's hard to be anything but excited with thirty-plus children all so happy to be at their Christmas party. Some of the mums I'd got to know really well and they were all delighted with my news too.

I rang Mr Smith as soon as I got home and thanked him (probably a bit too much). Cliff and I knew he had gone out of his way to help us. I also bombarded him with questions.

"What day was best to start? What uniform did Jamie need? What time should he be there, all day or half day to start with? Should he be dinners or sandwiches?"

He was relaxed – and very patient – with every answer. He made it clear we should do what suited Jamie. If we felt Jamie should do half days for a while, that was fine. If Jamie wanted to have dinners one day, just bring in the dinner money. If Jamie wanted to go back after half term to say goodbye to his friends at his current school, that was fine.

This left me feeling very strange. I was so used to having meeting upon meeting about every part of Jamie's school life this was alien to me. But it was a good strange feeling.

Picking Jamie up from school that afternoon was a strain. He didn't know this was going to be his last day. I got the impression most of the staff didn't know either (the head had only found out that morning as well). His SA had been told, as had his teacher obviously. I'd gone in a little earlier to thank them for their support (I'm nothing if not polite) and his SA in particular was really sad to say goodbye. The other children were told Jamie wasn't going to come back and there were a few tears from a couple of the girls. Jamie seemed to pick up on the situation, but didn't get at all upset. He gave his SA a hug and when I reminded him it was the school disco that night they both broke in to a rendition of their favourite song together, including all the dance moves.

"Oh, oh, oh," Jamie sang, leaning as far back as he could without falling over. 'Low' was the song she used all the time to get him moving and I felt really sad we were saying goodbye to a really supportive − and fun − person. We said we'd keep in touch.

At the disco that evening, I told a few of the other class mums who were mostly surprised and said Jamie would be missed. True to form, Jamie was the first on the dance floor and knew all the moves to all the dances. Dressed in his favourite smart shirt and chinos he ran around getting everyone from the youngest to the oldest to dance with him. No one can resist that boy on the dance floor. I felt a pang of guilt and regret. Would he miss the friends he'd made? Was it the right thing to do?

"You okay, Jo?" George's mum asked as she came over to where I was stood watching Jamie and George dancing together.

"Ah, I'm just hoping we've made the right decision, that Jamie won't miss out on things like this," I replied, shrugging.

"It's the school that's missing out, Jo, not Jamie. It's such a shame, but it's their loss."

She was right. The decision had been made. Jamie − we − were starting a new chapter. One where Jamie could feel he belonged.

CHAPTER 20

NEW BEGINNINGS

The Christmas holidays flew by and before we knew it Jamie was starting at his new school. Cliff and I went with him on his first day. Wearing modern black rectangular glasses and his spikey blonde hair, he looked very grown up in his grey trousers, white shirt and new blue and silver-grey striped school tie. Luckily for us it was the type of tie that didn't need tying as it was attached with elastic – we could save that new skill for when he was older.

His class teacher, Mrs B, and Mr Smith both came out to welcome him and he was taken into his class. We followed like extras. An eager classmate showed Jamie where to put his coat and bag. He seemed fine. In fact, he seemed more aware of what was going on than we had given him credit for. We left him sitting with the rest of his class on the brightly coloured carpet playing with some dinosaurs.

I spent the rest of the day at home not really doing anything, but keeping busy. After picking Louise up from playschool we pottered around and she kept me distracted with her chatter about her princess dolls. That Christmas had seen her collection of Disney dolls grow and she liked nothing better than to get them all out, dress up in her golden yellow Belle dress and dance with them. Flicking her shoulder length shiny dark bobbed hair and grinning at me as she skipped and twirled around I was grateful for her happy spirit. When I went to collect him, he came skipping – yes, skipping – out. I know it sounds clichéd, but it's true. His teacher told me it was as if he'd been there forever. He was happy. That was clear.

After the first, very uneventful week, Jamie seemed settled. The only downside to him being at this school was I was having to drive him to and from school every day. Although only fifteen minutes away by car it meant a lot of juggling and for the first few weeks I muddled by.

Sam was more than okay letting himself into the house. Of course, at almost 11 years old and now at senior school he was more than happy to have a bit more independence. He had started senior school the previous September and was a typical pre-teen in many ways, taking more interest in his hair, what he wore and wanting to go out with his friends more. He still was a lovely young man to have around and I loved our times we spent together. Going to see a musical every summer had become a tradition and it was this love of all things musical that had got him his coveted place at the school when he'd auditioned for their performing arts programme.

Trying to get Louise to playschool, check Sam was getting off to school and run Jamie to school was no mean feat. Often, we'd make it into playschool just as the other children were all sitting down for registration.

Jamie's new school was outside of the designated distance so I had been advised the council could provide a mini bus or a private taxi (shared) for him to get to school. Following another madly rushed morning I realised I was being over controlling again and called the transport office to enquire about school transport. As Jamie was only eight, they agreed that a private taxi would be best rather than a larger mini bus that went to a number of other places en route. They told me he would have an 'escort' with him in the taxi and would share the taxi with another girl who also attended the school. Although I was nervous, it all sounded perfect, and with the grand prix-like driving I could end up displaying if I carried on, I agreed to give it a go.

The following Monday morning we – Cliff, me and Jamie – stood outside the house at the allotted time and the taxi arrived.

"Hello, you must be Jamie. Lovely to meet you," said the lady who got out of the back seat. "I'm Eileen, you are going to come along with me to school today, aren't you?" She was an elderly woman, who looked like a typical grandma with short, grey hair, set in a semi perm, very small – tiny in fact – with a well-worn face beaming at Jamie. Then the driver wound down his window and also introduced himself.

"Don't worry, Mum, we'll take good care of him. See you after school, we'll drop him off right at the door. Come on then Jamie, let's go get Anna."

With that Jamie happily got in the car and they drove away. It was as simple as that.

Well, for Jamie it was as simple as that. For me it wasn't. I felt pretty lost. Like most parents feel when they are waving their child off on their first day of school. Cliff couldn't understand why I was so jittery.

"I'm really worried about him," I explained as we went back in to the house.

"What? Why? He was more than happy when he left," was Cliff's confused response.

Clearly, he was not getting this at all.

"Do you think he knew what was going on? How do we know the taxi driver will drive safely? Will Eileen make sure he gets into his classroom, not just drop him off somewhere outside the school? How will we know he arrived there safely? Then what about after school? Will the teacher take him to the car? Will he be upset I'm not there?"

Cliff tried not to laugh at me overworrying. He'd got used to my need to be in control, especially when it came to Jamie's safety.

"It'll be fine Jo. They do this all the time. They will have a plan in place. Call the school if you're really worried, but I think he'll be absolutely fine."

Before I had a chance to though, Mrs B had texted me – without my asking – to reassure me he was there safe and sound.

Later that morning, after I'd taken Louise to playschool, on time and without rushing I thought about my concerns with the taxi. It was the letting go. I knew my role was changing. Jamie was becoming a little more independent. I was finally letting go of some of the control – and that was hard. For so long I had had to do everything and here was someone else stepping in and saying they could help. In fact, more than that, here were lots of people who knew what they were doing and offering to help. I wasn't used to it.

Jamie revelled in this little bit of independence. That afternoon, he came home holding Eileen's hand and quite happy chatting about 'kool' and singing a song he'd learnt

And so the weeks went on and Jamie settled in to his new school. He seemed to have made friends. He talked about making toast, going to the shops and loved dance club. A lady who worked as a therapist at the school and who lived around the corner even offered to bring him home after dance club. It was all so easy, and so relaxed.

I didn't need to go into school to discuss Jamie's participation in after-school clubs. There were no notes in his communication book about what Jamie had and hadn't achieved that day. In fact, I was in the dark quite a lot. But I learned to accept this and trust the school. Trust they knew what they were doing and they were doing the best for Jamie. In my heart, I know they were. When Jamie came home and gave us a perfect rendition of *Mamma Mia* (signs included) they had learned in assembly that day, when he asked if Mary could come around and watch *Barney*, when he asked if there was school tomorrow without any worry in his voice. I knew we had made the right decision. Moving on and letting go. It was for the best, but it was hard.

~

Jamie spent the next four years at Treetops and whilst he never made huge leaps academically we could always tell he felt 'part' of things. It was during his time here that we said goodbye to Geraldine, as speech therapy came as part of the daily routine. She did a fantastic handover and we put our trust in the school speech therapist. No school is perfect and Treetops had its faults but he was included in everything from school plays to dance competitions and was given opportunities to flourish in many ways. There's a lot to be said for feeling like you belong somewhere. He would talk about the friends he made there for years after.

Then, when Jamie was thirteen he left Treetops. Sam was sixteen and had just finished at 'senior' school and it was two days after Lou's ninth birthday, when we all moved to Singapore. But that's a whole other story.

~

AFTERWORD

Ordinary fears

"What keeps you awake at night?"

This was a topic that came up one week at a creative writing course I'd joined. Over coffee the next day with a group of friends, I asked them the same question and it was clear that, as parents, our biggest fears are for our children. We all talked about wanting to protect our loved ones from the unknown menace that lies in wait. The paedophiles we constantly read about, rapists who prey on teenage girls and the mugger out to make a quick buck. But, actually for me, these are not the fears that keep me awake.

I'm quite a positive thinker generally so try not to spend time worrying about things I can't control, but when you have children there is a part of you that takes on more responsibility for worrying it seems. Having been told to write something about the subject made me really consider what it was that kept me awake.

I realised it wasn't if we have enough money to pay the mortgage each month – money doesn't control my happiness. I know that's easy to say when you can pay your mortgage, but I believe I have made choices in my life that meant I didn't have to worry about this. I didn't worry about war – although that scared me, especially as the 9/11 attacks had recently happened, but this was something completely out of my hands and so there was little point wasting my worry time.

For me, my greatest fears were my children wouldn't live their lives to the fullest. Each fear is slightly different for each child, and yet tied with a common bond.

They would be led astray by friends who would introduce them to drugs, drink or worse. They would fall into a job they loathed and spend their days wishing they could leave. I worry Sam wouldn't see what I see – his sensitive nature, his spark of independence already waiting to burst into flames, his sharp humour that could take him far if he used it well. For Lou, my fears were that she could pass the bias that stops so many women reaching their potential. That she feels she can and should achieve as much as any man.

I hope they don't settle down too early, and know it's okay to have a career and really care about it. I worry they will grow up hating the way they look as so many young adults do now. I worry they will have their hearts broken once too many times. I worry they won't ever have their hearts broken and so never feel those all-important emotions. I hope they will never give up on their dreams.

But these worries still don't keep me awake really. They may taunt me at times but I try to be rational and remember we are bringing our children up to be open minded, go-getting, can-do people of the world. Hopefully this leads them to all of the things they want and desire.

Then I dig deeper and realise these same fears are more complex with Jamie. I fear he will not be accepted fully into the adult world. I worry he doesn't have the same choices as his brother and sister. I fear he will work in a supermarket – a token gesture by a huge company who has to tick the right boxes – not because he was seen as someone that could offer their company anything or because he wants to work there. I fear he will not find love. Or he won't be loved as we all hope to be loved. True, deep, caring, lusty love. That he won't be 'allowed' to commit through marriage if he wants to, the same as you or I can. My fears are he will always feel like he is on the outside looking in – at a world that talks the talk but can't walk the walk.

The worry Jamie will spend his life looking up at a glass ceiling that is really made of solid steel for him. How will he ever break through? I worry his potential lies more in the hands of others than it does in his own. He has so much more to prove, so many more hills to climb. He needs others to be more understanding, more patient and have more awareness – I fear that is asking the impossible. That is a fear that will not go away.

I have similar fears for all my children, but those for Jamie feel more out of my control. While I may be able to help build his confidence to live independently, it's the system we are reliant on to offer him a safe place to live. While I can encourage him to make relationships, society as a whole has to get over their fear and prejudice about him falling in love and having a full and healthy relationship – yes including sex. I can encourage him to get a job he really wants to do, but I can't make employers make those jobs open to him.

I worry about a future when Cliff and I are not around to support and fight his corner with him. I hope when the time comes he is ready to stand on his own. If he isn't, I hope he gets the support and encouragement he needs.

That's what keeps me awake at night.

EMPLOYMENT STATISTICS

There's light at the end of the tunnel!

According to an online national survey carried out in America in 2015, only fifty-seven per cent of the 511 adults with Down syndrome were employed. Although this sounds like a lot, the majority were largely employed in jobs that under-utilise their skills. It showed most adults with Down syndrome worked in a limited number of job categories, referred to as the five Fs: Food (fast food and kitchen work), Filth (cleaning and janitorial services), Flowers (florists and landscaping), Factories (light assembly line work) and Filing (office mail delivery), even though a large majority (sixty-nine per cent) of adults reported they use computers. Also, it's worth noting only three per cent of that figure were employed (and paid) full time.

Source Article: Kumin, L., & Schoenbrodt, L. (2015). Employment in Adults with Down Syndrome in the United States: Results from a National Survey. Journal of Applied Research in Intellectual Disabilities.

Hopefully the future will look brighter as more employers reach out to young adults with special needs and more advocates such as the Down Syndrome Association push for better opportunities. The DSA want to move away from the concept of 'giving people something to do' to an approach that progresses employees towards new outcomes, through training, confidence building and skills development. As such it has begun something called Workfit that is a tailored service dedicated to training employers about the Down syndrome learning profile. It aims to find the right employment opportunities, for the right people. A step in the right direction at least!

Changes in me

Becoming a parent changes everybody without question. You grow as a person, learn things about yourself, and develop a bond with your child that can take your breath away. Your life suddenly becomes less selfish.

Becoming a parent of a child with special needs does all of that, and some other stuff you had no idea about. It has changed me in ways I could never have anticipated that day I got the phone call telling me the test was positive. That day I felt my world change for sure. My whole being took on emotions I didn't know existed, some of which would not surface for years. The feeling of protectiveness most mothers feel for their unborn child became more intense, and of course the sadness of what we were told overwhelmed me.

But every year I feel differently. Each milestone feels different. Having Jamie is different.

I can gloss over difficult feelings and put aside anxiety for long periods if necessary. However, I have learned at some point they have to be addressed. There have been pivotal points over the years where I have had to take stock of what I am feeling and deal with it. Usually this manifests itself in the form of sadness and sometimes anger. Something will trigger a flood of tears I didn't know had been pushing at the backs of my eyes for months. A flippant comment by somebody will provoke feelings I'd been putting to one side and lead to days of anxiety. Writing a book about something would lead to years of soul searching!

When Sam first said 'Mummy', I was delighted. When Jamie said 'Mummy', I was equally delighted and yet painfully aware of how much longer it took. The fact he then went on to call me *'aahdee'* for over a year just added to the fun and frustration. I have learned to appreciate stuff other parents probably take for granted.

For example, when Jamie learnt to jump. After years of physiotherapy and occupational therapy appointments I knew how bloody hard it was for Jamie to jump. You watch any two-year-old try to jump. They are comical in their attempts, bending down and with great effort, launching themselves up – only for their feet to stay firmly planted on the ground. But, very soon, those feet are lifting and before you know – or even realise – it those feet leave the ground.

Karen and I both laugh fondly when we remember how, at developmental group as two-year-olds, they would both try their hardest to get their feet to do what they were supposed to, often falling over in the process. When Jamie finally did it, at three years old, we were both so proud of him. Then, months later, I can still remember the day Karen told me Holly could jump – we were both so excited – as was Holly, who proudly showed off her jumping. Small things mean a lot.

I have had conversations with other parents who were worried their child wasn't doing so well at school. That their son only got nine out of ten on their spelling test the previous week. Asking me if I thought they should go and see the teacher as 'they don't want them being in the low set'. No, those parents never saw the irony of what they were saying.

When Jamie was in mainstream school, at the gates, as mums do, notes were compared about what books were being read, if homework was being done and so on. I'd always smile politely if I was asked directly if I thought the books were too easy or the homework enough. They clearly didn't realise Jamie was still learning the basics of reading and so didn't get the same books, and his homework was more of a 'let's see if we can get him to hold the pencil right tonight'.

Sometimes I would get angry at those parents, who really didn't appreciate how easy it was for them. I know that sounds very self-centred, but it happened so often. Children who were doing perfectly well at school being pushed so hard they no longer enjoyed learning.

When Jamie was born, as new parents we felt lost at sea, not sure which way to swim to reach the shore. We relied on professionals to give us advice and trusted Jamie would be given the best possible care. We quickly learned this wasn't the case and so became Jamie's lighthouse as it were. I don't let doctors tell me what Jamie can and can't do, or education professionals tell me where Jamie will go to school. I argue, I discuss, I leave our – and his – options open. I learn more about things.

If you speak to any parent of a child with special needs – especially those whose children are doing better than expected – you will hear fighting talk. A parent who hasn't sat back and said okay, my child only has *this* much potential. Parents who see potential far beyond those the system thought possible.

One of the many good things that have come about as a result of being Jamie's mum is the amazing people I have met through and because of him. I'm in constant admiration of those parents whose child's disability or difficulties mean a constant (and I mean constant, twenty-four hour) day – those who take turns sleeping. Those parents who have had to watch their child go through major surgery or illness, and yet they are still smiling. I have a huge amount of respect for parents who have made a difference to the help and support our children receive by not accepting the services – and predictions – that were offered to them ten or twenty years ago.

I have feelings I don't know how to describe for those parents who have lost their children after all the fighting they have done on their behalf. Many of them carry on fighting for children like their own. Believe me, these parents don't worry about spelling tests.

Patience is the most relied on change in me as a person. Before Jamie, I would say I had average patience. Now I'd say I have the patience of twenty saints! But not always!

I have quite calmly found a video among a pile, put it on the television, heard Jamie's 'not that one' put it back and tried the next one thirty times in one morning. I learned he needed to see the opening few seconds before he was sure. I knew the routine. Of course, I would get frustrated, but I realised running out of patience didn't help, so I went with it. I learned when Jamie was pushing it and will be as patient as I need to be.

I have explained to him repeatedly what is happening after breakfast every day and still when he says, *"kool?"* I'll reply "Yes, school today" like it was the first time he asked.

Patience leads to frustration sometimes and I have to rein myself in.

'I know he can read these bloody words so why won't he just say them?' I have said to myself while we were reading his schoolbook and I point to the words 'Mum' and 'Dad' and he says '*Barney*'.

He knew I knew he knew, he knew I want him to know, he knew I'd be getting fed up. Oh, he knew!

At times like that I had to laugh (to myself of course) and not to worry. He would get there when he was ready to – or when he thought we had waited long enough.

If you had asked me pre-kids if I could be that patient I would have said no, definitely not.

If you'd asked ten years ago, would I have thought he'd be reading at all at seven, I would have said no – after all that's what the doctor told us.

Sometimes things do become too much and there are a number of ways I've learnt to cope with this. I run away – usually just for a night out or for a chat over a cuppa with close friends. Cliff and I try to give each other proper space when we can, maybe a weekend away without the children or just a few hours on our own in the house. I write, which always helps me relax and I love to write long emails to friends who are far away.

I know I have to make time to be just me. I also know I have to give Jamie time to be just him. That's taken me a long time to learn. The same for Louise and Sam; they need space away from his singing, dancing, general Jamie-ness and he from them. We've all as a family learnt to adapt to each other, that's what families do.

If you'd asked me ten years ago would Jamie be the cheeky, amazingly empathic, funny, talented, sometimes pain-in-the-arse little boy he became, I wouldn't have known if that was possible, but I'd have been optimistic.

I didn't know then his personality was going to be quite so multifaceted. After all, the doctor told us he would still be in nappies, not talking much and probably quite sickly with very few social skills and not much of a life. When I end another week of football, drama, dancing, friends over, homework, parties, family rows, new milestones and am totally exhausted. I know.

That we've all changed!

The future

I spend a lot of time not thinking about the future. It's too hard, and too complicated. It's inevitable. It is coming and there's nothing I can do. I have warmed up, been on the starting blocks, and heard the gun and ...

Bang. I heard the B.
I should be following the 'plan'.
All good athletes plan their race, don't they?
BUT. What if the race changes?
I thought I was running a middle distance.
I would start well; keep some of my reserves for the final push at the end and all that.

But it turns out I'm in for the long distance. A marathon.
Have to make other plans I guess.
Have to have good pace, know when to push forward and when to hold back.
Shit, must sort out a plan.

I've never been a huge planner. You know, the sort of thing organised people do — have a five-year plan.

When we think about the future how many of us consider the fact our children may still be at home with us when we retire? Yes, we may joke they'll never fly the nest, laugh they've got it easy living at home. But really, how often does that happen?

When we think about the future, how many of us dream about our child's wedding? The teary-eyed mum, waving a fond farewell to the child they are losing and a wary hello to the child they are gaining?

When we think about the future how many of us dream of our children gaining degrees at university and becoming a doctor, teacher, great artist?

I have those dreams, ideals, and hopes for all my children. I truly do. But I'm a realist as well.

What I spend a lot of time *not* thinking about is how can I dream of Jamie's wedding day when I know society just can't get its head around the fact he'll find love in the same way Sam and Lou will. It is possible he will find a lovely young girl who happens to have an extra chromosome the same as him, who will understand him and love him. Possible, but not certain. If not, will a neuro-typical young girl fall in love with him? Will he experience the heart-wrenching moments of shall I, shan't I kiss her? Does she want me to phone or should I play it cool? Would a neuro-typical girl even give him the time of day? Will he ever lose his virginity? Will that occasion be something he even understands if it happens? What if he wants to have children of his own? Still a subject most refuse to discuss. There are men who have Down syndrome who have fathered children but they are extremely rare.

As for Jamie's career, I find that hard to think about because it leads to so much frustration. Given the right help, resources and support I am sure he could enter the world of work. But, in reality I see the lack of help, resources and support and find it almost impossible to accept his greatest goal may be to work at the local supermarket. Of course, I have the utmost respect for those young adults with Down syndrome who do. God knows, they have had to work harder than most to get there.

Many would say good for the supermarkets. Rubbish! Sadly, more often than not they are just ticking the boxes they have to tick. How many of those employees with Down syndrome are promoted to store manager or even department head?

~

I find it hard to be happy about the imaginary pat on the head some supermarket manager will give Jamie one day when he deigns to give him a job he is more than capable of doing.

~

The thought of Jamie living at home when he is thirty doesn't thrill me, but we have already *not* thought about it. We purposely consider houses big enough to accommodate a separate living area. I'd rather that than he was in a communal house pretending to be independent, while relying on social services to send someone round three times a day to check he hasn't burnt the house down while making his lunch.

If he were to decide he'd like to leave home and live on his own (or share a house with others) I'd support him. I'd be overjoyed. If it were his choice; if he chose his house, he bought the furniture and had a say on how it was decorated. Not given a council-approved house that had been specially bought for 'his sort'. But, again, as a realist I have to accept he may live in such a place and I will try to be happy for him if *he* decided he wanted to live there.

It is because of these issues I fight for inclusion. Not just within education. The more Jamie is included in normal, everyday things other children and young adults do, the more society will learn acceptance and understanding. However, this isn't easy. When Jamie joined our local Beavers group, I was asked to stay with him, as they didn't have enough adults to manage a child with special needs. I was annoyed about this as none of the other boys had their mum there every week. They also had made a quick assumption about Jamie, without actually getting to know him. But I could accept he did need someone there on occasions. The problem was, what do I do with Sam and Lou? Luckily, my mum helped and started going along with him. But when the group swapped days and Mum was unable to take him due to other commitments, Jamie had to leave. So, he missed out.

I felt it was important Jamie went to clubs like Beavers. But the reality was we couldn't just sign him up, take him along, and leave him to have fun – as other parents could.

As he gets older, he should have the same opportunities his friends have to join a football team, after-school clubs and go out and play on his bike. But, as ever these things are not as straightforward.

So, to think about college, work, adulthood, seems a long way off.

All of these things are ifs and buts anyway.

If Jamie gets the right kind of support.

If Jamie reaches the type of independence we hope he will.

If Jamie meets the person who was meant to be for him.

But …

And that's what I spend a lot of time not thinking about.

Time to stop

Many years ago, when I first started writing this book I didn't know where I was going with it, or what I wanted to get from it. In a way, it has been forced out of me – albeit in an encouraging way. But I also know it was something that needed to be done.

The problem then (and has been for a while now) was stopping. To end it felt like saying, "So that's it, that's us. That is life with a child who has Down syndrome."

But it's not. It is still changing. I'm still learning. Jamie still surprises us all.

When Jamie turned eight, I felt I had said enough. On that first family trip to Singapore I felt I'd reached the end of my story – or at least the one I wanted to tell. Certainly, a lot happened in that year.

He had settled into his new school and was making steady progress. One day, he even came home with a special piece of yellow card. That piece of yellow card made me cry – with pride, and relief. On it he had written his name – himself. A major achievement, and one I, and his teachers, had thought would not happen (or not for a long time anyway).

He had learned to take himself to the toilet and accidents had become rare.

He had even begun to cope with sleeping in his own bed occasionally – and we had really given up on that one. Okay, so we still had to get up for him every night, but he went back to his bed most times without an almighty fight. That was a major breakthrough.

He had joined a football team and played in his first tournament. Had progressed with his dancing and been on stage tap dancing! He still loved his cricket.

He was communicating his feelings better (sometimes too well) so there was less frustration. His speech was improving so much that I had less worries about him not being understood.

I still felt guilt. Guilt I didn't do enough. Enough reading, spelling or maths practice with him. Guilt I should have pushed harder for services, help and support. Guilt I was too soft on him. Guilt I was too hard on him. A lot of worry I didn't understand where he was coming from sometimes.

I also felt guilty Sam and Lou were missing out. Just by writing about it, Jamie was taking up more time. I wondered if they resented the fact I wasn't writing a book about life with them. After all, they are just as special.

I didn't know the answers. I just hoped we all would get as much from reading this as I had writing it.

Then there was all the stuff I wanted to say and hadn't. What is it like for my parents? How do they feel about having a grandson like Jamie? Do they worry? Do they think we cope? How has having a child with special needs affected my relationship with Cliff?

But it had been a good year. I felt it was time to stop.

I knew Jamie would carry on learning, developing and becoming more independent. I, as his mum, would keep on encouraging, helping and nagging. We, as a family, would keep on changing.

So, I planned to finish my story there.

But then, before I realised, Jamie was turning ten and I was *still* not quite done. Having looked back over what I'd written, I decided maybe I should try to publish our story. I read and re-read, dissected and deliberated. I added bits that were too important to miss out – like moving to a special needs school. I tried not to take away from it too much. I thought then I would find my publisher and let this other baby go.

Silly me.

Jamie is now seventeen!

What? When did that happen?

For many reasons, some of which I'll probably never fully appreciate, I didn't let it go when Jamie turned ten. I wasn't ready. I kept the pages gathering dust on the bookshelf. I even took it with us to store on another bookshelf when we moved countries to live in Singapore when he was thirteen. I kept thinking I was ready to let it go but I wasn't.

Now I am. I really am. I'm sure I am.

Clearly a lot has changed between the ages of ten and seventeen and I seriously considered adding those missing seven years. But no, I decided that was a whole other story. A whole other book.

Now it really is time to stop. Time to let go of the past in some ways. Time to put it out there.

Time to move on. Time to share this part of our story. Who knew it would take this long? But, it's definitely time …

Mountain climbing

I feel like having a child with special needs is like climbing.

Sometimes it's like climbing Mount Everest. You know there's a peak and that is where you are determinedly headed. You know it's going to be tough but you will dig in and fight your way up there. But just when you thought you could see the top some bugger comes along with a different map to the one you were following and tells you you've got a long way to go and the weather is closing in. But what can you do, you're almost there?

So, you carry on climbing.

Other times it's more like climbing a mountain that slopes gently towards the sun. You stroll along, taking your time, aware you are out of breath, but enjoying the challenge. When you reach a part that feels like the top, you can stand there smugly and admire the view. Pitying those below rushing around, worrying about trivial matters and useless concerns.

I try to take in that 'view' quite often and relish it. I breathe in the clean air, let the rays warm me to the bone, relax and let go. Then I have to keep on keeping on.

When I first thought about publishing this book I assumed

it would only appeal to parents or families who have a child with Down syndrome. I hoped it would be a story they could relate to; laughing at the familiarity of awkward situations and sympathising with the trials and tribulations I wrote about.

I wanted it to lead to a better understanding of what having Down syndrome means.

I hoped it would inspire new parents, and those who have older children and even those whose children are all grown up. I would love it to give some hope to those who have just had a 'positive test' for Down syndrome. That they take that positive literally and not be pushed in to a decision they might regret.

Having let it rest for some time I can see many different people could get something from reading it too. Anyone who has a child – 'normal' or otherwise. Anyone who works with children. Those who have an interest in how people – and families in particular – interact. It is about the reality that is family life. And everyone likes to know how others do it. I can't be the only nosey person in the world. Can I?!

I hope it helps others realise that while having that extra chromosome does make someone 'different', it really doesn't mean they can't fit in. Whatever that may mean.

Children are the same whatever their ability – they all get upset, they all get angry, they all have their strengths and weaknesses and they all annoy the hell out of their parents.
After reading it, if one person takes the time to listen when a child with speech problems stumbles over their words, and doesn't interrupt or talk for them. If one person thinks to learn to

use sign language. When a friend with a child who has special needs has to cancel at the last minute AGAIN, if someone understands, then I feel I will have achieved something. If just a handful of people explain to their children patience really is a virtue, and they in turn, wait for their classmate to catch up.

Then I will know I've hit the spot.

DON'T SCREEN US OUT!

Something else happened in between writing and publishing my story. Something uglier and more worrying than anything I'd come across. Politicians and the medical profession – those people we trust to do what's best for us – began talking about introducing new prenatal screening as standard to all pregnant women. Let there be no sugar coating. This new screening process is fundamentally going to mean the eradication of Down syndrome. Whilst at the time of printing this book it was only being offered to those 'deemed to have a high chance of carrying a child with Down syndrome', due to its hype it's likely that more women will take up screening, and, if high abortion rates persist, more babies will be aborted. Leading to a 'profound long-term effect' on the Down syndrome community.

If you are a parent reading this whose child doesn't have Down syndrome let me explain how this feels to me …

Let's say your child wears glasses and therefore you have to take him or her to the optician regularly. Yes, it's a pain having to make an appointment and go there, especially as you know there are other children that don't wear glasses. But it's okay, you've got used to the idea and anyway, your child isn't in pain, hurting anyone because of their glasses or causing themselves any harm.

Now imagine the doctors and those who make the laws told you they had come up with a test to screen out children that may need glasses before they are even born and will be doing so with immediate effect. Without consulting you – a parent of a child wearing glasses and therefore probably quite a good source of information – or your child, who wears the glasses. Instead, these people talk about how really clever they are having found a way to detect the gene that causes the eyes to not be perfect.

I know this may sound very far-fetched. But maybe they'll find that gene one day. Then what?

I'd also urge you to think about those people in Iceland who have Down syndrome. Imagine how they feel living in a country where the government has made them feel they are not worthy of life.

Since introducing the tests in the early 2000s **NO CHILDREN IN ICELAND ARE KNOWINGLY BORN WITH DOWN SYNDROME.**

That means every single person who had the test, decided to abort.

Shame on you, Iceland!

If one person agrees with me that more money should be spent on helping children with Down syndrome once they are born – and not on eradicating them before they have a chance to prove themselves – and that person picks up a pen and writes to their local MP and signs the Don't Screen Us Out petition then this whole, often painful process of writing my story, will have achieved something.

I urge you to learn what this really means. Don't believe the hype.

For more information visit *dontscreenusout.org*.

FURTHER READING AND RESOURCES

Websites that I have found useful:

Down Syndrome Research Foundation: *www.dsrf.org/about-us*
Down Syndrome International: *www.dseinternational.org/en-us*
Down's Syndrome Association: *www.downs-syndrome.org.uk*
Don't Screen Us Out campaign: *www.savingdownsyndrome.org*
The National Down Syndrome Society: *www.ndss.org/about-down-syndrome/down-syndrome*
The Circles Concept: *www.ascd.org/ascd/pdf/journals/ed_lead/el_199109_walker-hirsch.pdf*
Health-related issues: *www.ds-health.com*
National Center on Health, Physical Activity and Disability (NCHPAD):
   www.nchpad.org;
   www.nchpad.org/1415/6299/Employment~in~Adults~with~Down~Syndrome
   www.langdondownmuseum.org.uk/dr-john-langdon-down
   www.lejeunefoundation.org
Picture Exchange Communication System (PECS): *www.pecsusa.com/pecs*
Signalong: *www.signalong.org.uk*
Special Needs and Parents (SNAP): *www.snapcharity.org*
Statements and the like in the UK: *www.gov.uk/children-with-special-educational-needs/extra-SEN-help*
Workfit: *www.dsworkfit.org.uk*

Books I have found helpful:

Teaching Children with Down Syndrome about Their Bodies, Boundaries, and Sexuality, A Guide for Parents and Professionals **by Terri Couwenhoven, M.S. Published by Woodbine House. ISBN-10: 189062733X/ ISBN-13: 978-189062733**

Blue Sky July **by Nia Wynn. Published by Seren Books/Penguin. ISBN-10: 0141037180/ ISBN-13: 978-0141037189**

NOT THE CROCODILE BOOK!

ABOUT THE AUTHOR

Joanne began her career in the late 1980s early 1990s writing about homes and interiors for women's magazines (a subject she previously had no 'professional' knowledge of). She credits her success at managing this to two things – a good nose for research and a love of stylish homes.

For fifteen years she worked full time as a writer and sub-editor before going freelance when her eldest child was born. When son number two arrived, her path changed slightly and she briefly dabbled in the world of playgroups and also trained as a Signalong tutor, which she taught to children and adults. When her daughter was born, these two new career paths fitted her life perfectly.

In between children she continued to write, including starting a blog and writing short stories. When she and her family moved to Singapore in 2014 she returned to freelancing, setting up her own company, Pasquale Publishing. Joanne's most recent work includes travel features, guides to things to do in Singapore, features for expat websites, website content for local artists and editing a book for a French 'nose'.

Throughout this time, she has continued to write fiction and has at least two stories 'on the go' at any time.

With a passion for travel, meeting people and tea she loves to combine the three when she can. She's also partial to a musical or two and is strangely obsessed with Billy Bragg. Family holidays are what keeps her motivated and as her children have grown she's discovered how much she still loves to travel on her own too. She is planning a book about the women of Bhutan, having visited and fallen in love with the country and its people. She's hoping this will develop in to a series looking at the lives and cultures of women around the world.

Her popular blog, *Five Go Mad in Singers* www.5gomad.com is about life as an expat in Singapore. The family plan to return to the UK in 2018 and Jo is hoping to continue blogging, writing and travelling, from a different perspective.

For more information on Jo and her work please visit:

www.apositiveresult.com
www.facebook.com/A-Positive-Result-229540890933660/
www.pasqualepublishing.com
Instagram @a_positive_result
Twitter.com/5gomadin

Summertime
Publishing

Springtime
Books

Also by Summertime Publishing and Springtime Books:

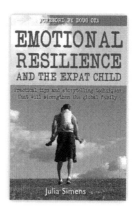